Diaspora: A Very Short Introduction

VERY SHORT INTRODUCTIONS are for anyone wanting a stimulating and accessible way in to a new subject. They are written by experts and have been published in more than 25 languages worldwide.

The series began in 1995 and now represents a wide variety of topics in history, philosophy, religion, science, and the humanities. The VSI library now contains more than 300 volumes—a Very Short Introduction to everything from ancient Egypt and Indian philosophy to conceptual art and cosmology—and will continue to grow in a variety of disciplines.

Very Short Introductions available now:

ADVERTISING Winston Fletcher
AFRICAN HISTORY
    John Parker and Richard Rathbone
AGNOSTICISM Robin Le Poidevin
AMERICAN HISTORY
    Paul S. Boyer
AMERICAN IMMIGRATION
    David A. Gerber
AMERICAN POLITICAL
    PARTIES AND ELECTIONS
    L. Sandy Maisel
AMERICAN POLITICS
    Richard M. Valelly
THE AMERICAN
    PRESIDENCY Charles O. Jones
ANAESTHESIA Aidan O'Donnell
ANARCHISM Colin Ward
ANCIENT EGYPT Ian Shaw
ANCIENT GREECE Paul Cartledge
ANCIENT PHILOSOPHY
    Julia Annas
ANCIENT WARFARE
    Harry Sidebottom
ANGELS David Albert Jones
ANGLICANISM Mark Chapman
THE ANGLO-SAXON AGE
    John Blair
THE ANIMAL KINGDOM
    Peter Holland

ANIMAL RIGHTS David DeGrazia
THE ANTARCTIC Klaus Dodds
ANTISEMITISM Steven Beller
ANXIETY Daniel Freeman and
    Jason Freeman
THE APOCRYPHAL GOSPELS
    Paul Foster
ARCHAEOLOGY Paul Bahn
ARCHITECTURE
    Andrew Ballantyne
ARISTOCRACY William Doyle
ARISTOTLE Jonathan Barnes
ART HISTORY Dana Arnold
ART THEORY Cynthia Freeland
ATHEISM Julian Baggini
AUGUSTINE Henry Chadwick
AUSTRALIA Kenneth Morgan
AUTISM Uta Frith
THE AVANT GARDE
    David Cottington
THE AZTECS Davíd Carrasco
BACTERIA Sebastian G. B. Amyes
BARTHES Jonathan Culler
BEAUTY Roger Scruton
BESTSELLERS John Sutherland
THE BIBLE John Riches
BIBLICAL ARCHAEOLOGY
    Eric H. Cline
BIOGRAPHY Hermione Lee

THE BLUES Elijah Wald
THE BOOK OF MORMON
    Terryl Givens
BORDERS Alexander C. Diener and
    Joshua Hagen
THE BRAIN Michael O'Shea
THE BRITISH
    CONSTITUTION
    Martin Loughlin
THE BRITISH EMPIRE
    Ashley Jackson
BRITISH POLITICS
    Anthony Wright
BUDDHA Michael Carrithers
BUDDHISM Damien Keown
BUDDHIST ETHICS
    Damien Keown
CANCER Nicholas James
CAPITALISM James Fulcher
CATHOLICISM Gerald O'Collins
THE CELL Terence Allen and
    Graham Cowling
THE CELTS Barry Cunliffe
CHAOS Leonard Smith
CHILDREN'S LITERATURE
    Kimberley Reynolds
CHINESE LITERATURE
    Sabina Knight
CHOICE THEORY
    Michael Allingham
CHRISTIAN ART Beth Williamson
CHRISTIAN ETHICS
    D. Stephen Long
CHRISTIANITY Linda Woodhead
CITIZENSHIP Richard Bellamy
CIVIL ENGINEERING
    David Muir Wood
CLASSICAL MYTHOLOGY
    Helen Morales
CLASSICS Mary Beard and
    John Henderson
CLAUSEWITZ Michael Howard
CLIMATE Mark Maslin

THE COLD WAR Robert McMahon
COLONIAL AMERICA
    Alan Taylor
COLONIAL LATIN AMERICAN
    LITERATURE Rolena Adorno
COMEDY Matthew Bevis
COMMUNISM Leslie Holmes
THE COMPUTER Darrel Ince
THE CONQUISTADORS
    Matthew Restall and
    Felipe Fernández-Armesto
CONSCIENCE Paul Strohm
CONSCIOUSNESS
    Susan Blackmore
CONTEMPORARY ART
    Julian Stallabrass
CONTINENTAL
    PHILOSOPHY Simon Critchley
COSMOLOGY Peter Coles
CRITICAL THEORY
    Stephen Eric Bronner
THE CRUSADES
    Christopher Tyerman
CRYPTOGRAPHY Fred Piper and
    Sean Murphy
THE CULTURAL
    REVOLUTION
    Richard Curt Kraus
DADA AND SURREALISM
    David Hopkins
DARWIN Jonathan Howard
THE DEAD SEA SCROLLS
    Timothy Lim
DEMOCRACY Bernard Crick
DERRIDA Simon Glendinning
DESCARTES Tom Sorell
DESERTS Nick Middleton
DESIGN John Heskett
DEVELOPMENTAL BIOLOGY
    Lewis Wolpert
THE DEVIL Darren Oldridge
DIASPORA Kevin Kenny
DICTIONARIES Lynda Mugglestone

DINOSAURS David Norman
DIPLOMACY Joseph M. Siracusa
DOCUMENTARY FILM
    Patricia Aufderheide
DREAMING J. Allan Hobson
DRUGS Leslie Iversen
DRUIDS Barry Cunliffe
EARLY MUSIC
    Thomas Forrest Kelly
THE EARTH Martin Redfern
ECONOMICS Partha Dasgupta
EDUCATION Gary Thomas
EGYPTIAN MYTH
    Geraldine Pinch
EIGHTEENTH-CENTURY
    BRITAIN Paul Langford
THE ELEMENTS Philip Ball
EMOTION Dylan Evans
EMPIRE Stephen Howe
ENGELS Terrell Carver
ENGINEERING David Blockley
ENGLISH LITERATURE
    Jonathan Bate
ENVIRONMENTAL
    ECONOMICS Stephen Smith
EPIDEMIOLOGY Rodolfo Saracci
ETHICS Simon Blackburn
THE EUROPEAN UNION
    John Pinder and Simon Usherwood
EVOLUTION Brian and
    Deborah Charlesworth
EXISTENTIALISM
    Thomas Flynn
FASCISM Kevin Passmore
FASHION Rebecca Arnold
FEMINISM Margaret Walters
FILM Michael Wood
FILM MUSIC Kathryn Kalinak
THE FIRST WORLD WAR
    Michael Howard
FOLK MUSIC Mark Slobin
FORENSIC PSYCHOLOGY
    David Canter

FORENSIC SCIENCE Jim Fraser
FOSSILS Keith Thomson
FOUCAULT Gary Gutting
FREE SPEECH Nigel Warburton
FREE WILL Thomas Pink
FRENCH LITERATURE
    John D. Lyons
THE FRENCH REVOLUTION
    William Doyle
FREUD Anthony Storr
FUNDAMENTALISM
    Malise Ruthven
GALAXIES John Gribbin
GALILEO Stillman Drake
GAME THEORY Ken Binmore
GANDHI Bhikhu Parekh
GENIUS Andrew Robinson
GEOGRAPHY John Matthews and
    David Herbert
GEOPOLITICS Klaus Dodds
GERMAN LITERATURE
    Nicholas Boyle
GERMAN PHILOSOPHY
    Andrew Bowie
GLOBAL CATASTROPHES
    Bill McGuire
GLOBAL ECONOMIC
    HISTORY Robert C. Allen
GLOBAL WARMING Mark Maslin
GLOBALIZATION Manfred Steger
THE GOTHIC Nick Groom
GOVERNANCE Mark Bevir
THE GREAT DEPRESSION
    AND THE NEW DEAL
    Eric Rauchway
HABERMAS
    James Gordon Finlayson
HAPPINESS Daniel M. Haybron
HEGEL Peter Singer
HEIDEGGER Michael Inwood
HERODOTUS Jennifer T. Roberts
HIEROGLYPHS Penelope Wilson
HINDUISM Kim Knott

HISTORY John H. Arnold
THE HISTORY OF
ASTRONOMY Michael Hoskin
THE HISTORY OF LIFE
Michael Benton
THE HISTORY OF
MATHEMATICS
Jacqueline Stedall
THE HISTORY OF MEDICINE
William Bynum
THE HISTORY OF TIME
Leofranc Holford-Strevens
HIV/AIDS Alan Whiteside
HOBBES Richard Tuck
HUMAN EVOLUTION
Bernard Wood
HUMAN RIGHTS
Andrew Clapham
HUMANISM Stephen Law
HUME A. J. Ayer
IDEOLOGY Michael Freeden
INDIAN PHILOSOPHY
Sue Hamilton
INFORMATION Luciano Floridi
INNOVATION Mark Dodgson
and David Gann
INTELLIGENCE Ian J. Deary
INTERNATIONAL
MIGRATION Khalid Koser
INTERNATIONAL
RELATIONS Paul Wilkinson
ISLAM Malise Ruthven
ISLAMIC HISTORY
Adam Silverstein
ITALIAN LITERATURE
Peter Hainsworth and David Robey
JESUS Richard Bauckham
JOURNALISM Ian Hargreaves
JUDAISM Norman Solomon
JUNG Anthony Stevens
KABBALAH Joseph Dan
KAFKA Ritchie Robertson
KANT Roger Scruton

KEYNES Robert Skidelsky
KIERKEGAARD Patrick Gardiner
THE KORAN Michael Cook
LANDSCAPES AND
GEOMORPHOLOGY
Andrew Goudie and Heather Viles
LANGUAGES Stephen R. Anderson
LATE ANTIQUITY Gillian Clark
LAW Raymond Wacks
THE LAWS OF
THERMODYNAMICS
Peter Atkins
LEADERSHIP Keith Grint
LINCOLN Allen C. Guelzo
LINGUISTICS Peter Matthews
LITERARY THEORY
Jonathan Culler
LOCKE John Dunn
LOGIC Graham Priest
MACHIAVELLI Quentin Skinner
MADNESS Andrew Scull
MAGIC Owen Davies
MAGNA CARTA Nicholas Vincent
MAGNETISM Stephen Blundell
MALTHUS Donald Winch
MAO Delia Davin
MARINE BIOLOGY
Philip V. Mladenov
THE MARQUIS DE SADE
John Phillips
MARTIN LUTHER
Scott H. Hendrix
MARTYRDOM Jolyon Mitchell
MARX Peter Singer
MATHEMATICS Timothy Gowers
THE MEANING OF LIFE
Terry Eagleton
MEDICAL ETHICS Tony Hope
MEDICAL LAW Charles Foster
MEDIEVAL BRITAIN
John Gillingham and
Ralph A. Griffiths
MEMORY Jonathan K. Foster

METAPHYSICS Stephen Mumford
MICHAEL FARADAY
    Frank A.J.L. James
MODERN ART David Cottington
MODERN CHINA Rana Mitter
MODERN FRANCE
    Vanessa R. Schwartz
MODERN IRELAND Senia Pašeta
MODERN JAPAN
    Christopher Goto-Jones
MODERN LATIN AMERICAN
    LITERATURE
    Roberto González Echevarría
MODERNISM Christopher Butler
MOLECULES Philip Ball
THE MONGOLS
    Morris Rossabi
MORMONISM
    Richard Lyman Bushman
MUHAMMAD
    Jonathan A.C. Brown
MULTICULTURALISM
    Ali Rattansi
MUSIC Nicholas Cook
MYTH Robert A. Segal
THE NAPOLEONIC WARS
    Mike Rapport
NATIONALISM Steven Grosby
NELSON MANDELA
    Elleke Boehmer
NEOLIBERALISM Manfred Steger
    and Ravi Roy
NETWORKS Guido Caldarelli and
    Michele Catanzaro
THE NEW TESTAMENT
    Luke Timothy Johnson
THE NEW TESTAMENT AS
    LITERATURE Kyle Keefer
NEWTON Robert Iliffe
NIETZSCHE Michael Tanner
NINETEENTH-CENTURY
    BRITAIN Christopher Harvie
    and H. C. G. Matthew

THE NORMAN CONQUEST
    George Garnett
NORTH AMERICAN
    INDIANS Theda Perdue and
    Michael D. Green
NORTHERN IRELAND
    Marc Mulholland
NOTHING Frank Close
NUCLEAR POWER Maxwell Irvine
NUCLEAR WEAPONS
    Joseph M. Siracusa
NUMBERS Peter M. Higgins
OBJECTIVITY Stephen Gaukroger
THE OLD TESTAMENT
    Michael D. Coogan
THE ORCHESTRA
    D. Kern Holoman
ORGANIZATIONS Mary Jo Hatch
PAGANISM Owen Davies
THE PALESTINIAN-ISRAELI
    CONFLICT Martin Bunton
PARTICLE PHYSICS Frank Close
PAUL E. P. Sanders
PENTECOSTALISM William K. Kay
THE PERIODIC TABLE
    Eric R. Scerri
PHILOSOPHY Edward Craig
PHILOSOPHY OF LAW
    Raymond Wacks
PHILOSOPHY OF SCIENCE
    Samir Okasha
PHOTOGRAPHY Steve Edwards
PLAGUE Paul Slack
PLANETS David A. Rothery
PLANTS Timothy Walker
PLATO Julia Annas
POLITICAL PHILOSOPHY
    David Miller
POLITICS Kenneth Minogue
POSTCOLONIALISM
    Robert Young
POSTMODERNISM
    Christopher Butler

POSTSTRUCTURALISM
    Catherine Belsey
PREHISTORY Chris Gosden
PRESOCRATIC PHILOSOPHY
    Catherine Osborne
PRIVACY Raymond Wacks
PROBABILITY John Haigh
PROGRESSIVISM Walter Nugent
PROTESTANTISM Mark A. Noll
PSYCHIATRY Tom Burns
PSYCHOLOGY Gillian Butler and
    Freda McManus
PURITANISM Francis J. Bremer
THE QUAKERS Pink Dandelion
QUANTUM THEORY
    John Polkinghorne
RACISM Ali Rattansi
RADIOACTIVITY Claudio Tuniz
RASTAFARI Ennis B. Edmonds
THE REAGAN REVOLUTION
    Gil Troy
REALITY Jan Westerhoff
THE REFORMATION
    Peter Marshall
RELATIVITY Russell Stannard
RELIGION IN AMERICA
    Timothy Beal
THE RENAISSANCE Jerry Brotton
RENAISSANCE ART
    Geraldine A. Johnson
RHETORIC Richard Toye
RISK Baruch Fischhoff and
    John Kadvany
RIVERS Nick Middleton
ROBOTICS Alan Winfield
ROMAN BRITAIN Peter Salway
THE ROMAN EMPIRE
    Christopher Kelly
THE ROMAN REPUBLIC
    David M. Gwynn
ROMANTICISM Michael Ferber
ROUSSEAU Robert Wokler
RUSSELL A. C. Grayling

RUSSIAN HISTORY
    Geoffrey Hosking
RUSSIAN LITERATURE
    Catriona Kelly
THE RUSSIAN REVOLUTION
    S. A. Smith
SCHIZOPHRENIA Chris Frith and
    Eve Johnstone
SCHOPENHAUER
    Christopher Janaway
SCIENCE AND RELIGION
    Thomas Dixon
SCIENCE FICTION David Seed
THE SCIENTIFIC
    REVOLUTION
    Lawrence M. Principe
SCOTLAND Rab Houston
SEXUALITY Véronique Mottier
SHAKESPEARE Germaine Greer
SIKHISM Eleanor Nesbitt
THE SILK ROAD James A. Millward
SLEEP Steven W. Lockley and
    Russell G. Foster
SOCIAL AND CULTURAL
    ANTHROPOLOGY
    John Monaghan and Peter Just
SOCIALISM Michael Newman
SOCIOLOGY Steve Bruce
SOCRATES C. C. W. Taylor
THE SOVIET UNION
    Stephen Lovell
THE SPANISH CIVIL WAR
    Helen Graham
SPANISH LITERATURE
    Jo Labanyi
SPINOZA Roger Scruton
SPIRITUALITY Philip Sheldrake
STARS Andrew King
STATISTICS David J. Hand
STEM CELLS Jonathan Slack
STUART BRITAIN John Morrill
SUPERCONDUCTIVITY
    Stephen Blundell

SYMMETRY Ian Stewart
TERRORISM Charles Townshend
THEOLOGY David F. Ford
THOMAS AQUINAS Fergus Kerr
THOUGHT Tim Bayne
TOCQUEVILLE Harvey C. Mansfield
TRAGEDY Adrian Poole
THE TROJAN WAR Eric H. Cline
TRUST Katherine Hawley
THE TUDORS John Guy
TWENTIETH-CENTURY
   BRITAIN Kenneth O. Morgan
THE UNITED NATIONS
   Jussi M. Hanhimäki
THE U.S. CONGRESS
   Donald A. Ritchie

THE U.S. SUPREME COURT
   Linda Greenhouse
UTOPIANISM
   Lyman Tower Sargent
THE VIKINGS Julian Richards
VIRUSES Dorothy H. Crawford
WITCHCRAFT Malcolm Gaskill
WITTGENSTEIN
   A. C. Grayling
WORK Stephen Fineman
WORLD MUSIC Philip Bohlman
THE WORLD TRADE
   ORGANIZATION
   Amrita Narlikar
WRITING AND SCRIPT
   Andrew Robinson

Available soon:

SOCIOLINGUISTICS
   John Edwards
MODERN WAR
   Richard English

MANAGEMENT
   John Hendry
FOOD
   John Krebs

For more information visit our web site

www.oup.co.uk/general/vsi/

Kevin Kenny

DIASPORA

A Very Short Introduction

OXFORD
UNIVERSITY PRESS

OXFORD
UNIVERSITY PRESS

Oxford University Press is a department of the University of Oxford.
It furthers the University's objective of excellence in research,
scholarship, and education by publishing worldwide.

Oxford   New York

Auckland   Cape Town   Dar es Salaam   Hong Kong   Karachi
Kuala Lumpur   Madrid   Melbourne   Mexico City   Nairobi
New Delhi   Shanghai   Taipei   Toronto

With offices in

Argentina   Austria   Brazil   Chile   Czech Republic   France   Greece
Guatemala   Hungary   Italy   Japan   Poland   Portugal   Singapore
South Korea   Switzerland   Thailand   Turkey   Ukraine   Vietnam

Oxford is a registered trademark of Oxford University Press
in the UK and certain other countries.

Published in the United States of America by
Oxford University Press
198 Madison Avenue, New York, NY 10016

Library of Congress Cataloging-in-Publication Data
Kenny, Kevin, 1960–
Diaspora : a very short introduction / Kevin Kenny.
p.   cm.
Includes index.
ISBN 978-0-19-985858-3 (pbk. : alk. paper)
1. Human beings—Migrations.
2. Emigration and immigration. 3. Transnationalism.
4. Culture and globalization. 5. Human geography. I. Title.
GN370.K46   2013
304.8—dc23   2012043546

7 9 8

Printed in Great Britain
by Ashford Colour Press Ltd., Gosport, Hants.
on acid-free paper

For Rosanna, Michelino, and Owen

Contents

List of illustrations xv

Acknowledgments xvii

1 What is diaspora? 1

2 Migration 16

3 Connections 40

4 Return 61

5 A global concept 87

6 The future of diaspora 105

Further reading 111

Index 115

List of illustrations

1   Detail from the Arch of Titus,
    81 CE **4**
    Copyright Antonella Merletto, by
    permission of the photographer

2   Slave market in Zanzibar,
    1872 **25**
    Picture Collection, the New York
    Public Library, Astor, Lenox, and
    Tilden Foundations

3   *Economic Pressure* by Seán
    Keating, 1936 **30**
    By permission of the Crawford Art
    Gallery, Cork, Ireland

4   Indian plantation worker in
    Sumatra, ca. 1900 **36**
    KITLV Digital Image Library, image
    code 78317

5   Chinese migrants in New York
    City, 1896 **51**
    Harper's Weekly, February
    29, 1896, Library of Congress,
    LC-USZ62-107167

6   David Ben-Gurion reads
    the Declaration of the
    Establishment of the State of
    Israel, 1948 **66**
    Photograph by Kluger Zoltan, State
    of Israel National Photo Collection,
    picture code D836-087

7   Palestinian women and
    children flee the town of Jaffa,
    1948 **68**
    Walid Khalidi, *A Photographic
    History of the Palestinians, 1876–1948*,
    Institute for Palestine Studies,
    photo 414

8   "Operation Solomon,"
    1991 **75**
    Photograph by Alpert Nathan, State
    of Israel National Photo Collection,
    picture code D205-101

9   Vietnamese refugees arrive in
    Malaysia, 1978 **93**
    Photograph by K. Gaugler, courtesy of
    United Nations High Commissioner
    for Refugees (UNHCR), image no.
    8268

10 Alvin Ailey American Dance
    Theater in Alvin Ailey's
    signature masterpiece
    Revelations **103**
    Photo by Nan Melville, courtesy of
    Alvin Ailey Dance Foundation, Inc.

Acknowledgments

I would like to thank Rosanna Crocitto, Mimi Cowan, Ian Delahanty, Robin Fleming, Hidetaka Hirota, Marjorie Howes, Dan Kanstroom, Bernie Kenny, Brian Malone, Gráinne McEvoy, Seth Meehan, Joe Nugent, Arissa Oh, Dana Sajdi, Rob Savage, Franziska Seraphim, Darius Szwarcewicz, Martin Summers, Steve West, and the members of the Seminar on Diaspora and Global Migration at Boston College. Their comments and criticisms, often stringent but always constructive, helped me articulate the argument in its final form. My research assistant Jooyeon Koo closely read successive drafts of each chapter, offered many helpful suggestions, and worked on the illustrations. Many thanks, finally, to Nancy Toff for inviting me to write the book and for editing the manuscript, and to Sonia Tycko and Joellyn Ausanka for managing the book's development from beginning to end.

Chapter 1
What is diaspora?

The word "diaspora" is everywhere. It is increasingly widespread in academic, journalistic, political, and popular usage. But what does diaspora mean? Until quite recently, the word had a specific and restricted meaning, referring principally to the dispersal and exile of the Jews. In the twentieth century, the meaning of the term gradually expanded to cover the involuntary dispersal of other populations, especially Armenians and people of African descent. Since the 1980s, diaspora has proliferated to a remarkable extent, to the point where it is now applied to migrants of almost every kind. But if diaspora is merely a synonym for migration, why is the word necessary? What does using the word explain?

Problems arise when diaspora is too rigidly defined, but also when its meaning its left open-ended. Diaspora is best approached not as a social entity that can be measured but as an idea that helps explain the world migration creates. As a concept, diaspora produces powerful insights into that world, but it can also produce some powerful distortions, depending on how the term is used and for what purpose. This book examines where the concept of diaspora came from, how its meaning changed over time, why its usage has expanded so dramatically in recent years, how it enables certain forms of political and cultural expression, and how it can both obscure and clarify the nature of human migration.

Origins

The Greek noun *diasporá* derives from the verb *diaspeirein*, a compound of "dia" (over or through) and "speirein" (to scatter or sow). The word emerged from the proto-Indo-European root, *spr*, which can be found today in such English words as "spore," "sperm," "spread," and "disperse." In all of its various uses, diaspora has something to do with scattering and dispersal. To the ancient Greeks, diaspora seems to have signified mainly a process of destruction. Epicurus used diaspora to refer to the decomposition of matter and its dissolution into smaller parts. Human communities subject to the destructive force of diaspora were similarly split asunder. Thucydides employed diaspora in this way, in a minor passage in the *History of the Peloponnesian War* (2:27), to describe the Athenians' destruction of Aegina and the banishment and dispersal of its people. Whereas Greek colonies retained close and mutually beneficial relations with their mother cities, the victims of diaspora enjoyed no such connections. In its original Greek sense, then, diaspora referred to a destructive process, rather than to a place, a group of people, or a benign pattern of population dispersal. It carried a distinctly negative—though not a religious—connotation, which differentiated it from other, more voluntary forms of population movement.

It was in Jewish history that diaspora assumed its most familiar form. The early parts of the Jewish story derive from biblical narratives, supported to some extent by archaeological evidence. Displacement, exile, and longing for a homeland were the central features of this narrative. The veracity of the Bible as history is not the issue here: the important point is that the history the Jews told to themselves, which still lies at the core of Jewish identity, was from the outset based on the idea of diaspora. Most accounts of the Jewish diaspora begin with the Babylonian captivity in 586 BCE. But according to the history related in the Bible, Jewish people had been migrating for centuries before that critical event.

The story of the earliest Jewish migrations is told in Genesis and Exodus. The Jewish people descended from Abraham, who led his followers from Babylonia (in present-day Iraq) to Canaan, which they named *Eretz Israel*, the land of Israel. Famine soon drove Abraham's descendants out of Canaan to Egypt, where Joseph, one of their kinsmen and an advisor to the pharaoh, welcomed them. Their position in Egypt gradually deteriorated until Moses, commanded by God to deliver the Hebrew people from slavery, led them back to Canaan. Moses caught a glimpse of the Promised Land before dying and, as subsequent books of the Hebrew Bible recount, his followers went on to build the nation of Israel, with the city of Jerusalem as its capital. The very earliest phase of Jewish history, then, involves the familiar cycle of migration, suffering, and return. One might even extend the story of exile all the way back to the expulsion of Adam and Eve.

The kingdom of Israel prospered under David and Solomon, but later split into two separate states, Israel to the north and Judah to the south. When the Assyrians invaded the Northern Kingdom in the eighth century, they destroyed the capital, Samara, and sent its leaders and some of its population into exile. Nebuchadnezzar II of Babylon conquered Judah in 586 BCE, destroyed the Temple in Jerusalem, and carried the Jewish elite back to Babylon. It was during this critical period of upheaval and exile just before and after the destruction of the Temple that Jewish leaders first wrote down their history, their law, and the tenets of their faith in a systematic manner. When the Persians took over the Babylonian Empire in 539 CE, many Jews returned to Judah. But the era of the Second Temple came to an end with the Roman conquest of Jerusalem in 70 CE, an event commemorated on the triumphal Arch of Titus, which still stands in Rome today. After a final Jewish revolt in 135 CE, the emperor Hadrian razed Jerusalem. From then until the foundation of the modern state of Israel in 1948, the Jewish people lacked an independent state.

The Greek words *diaspeirein* and *diasporá*, applied to Jewish history, came into widespread currency in the translation of the

1. **Detail from the Arch of Titus in Rome showing the menorah seized by the Romans after the destruction of the Second Temple in 70 CE.**

Hebrew scriptures known as the Septuagint (ca. 250 BCE). In this work, Jewish scholars based in Alexandria translated into Greek the books of Genesis, Exodus, Leviticus, Numbers, and Deuteronomy, which Christians later referred to as the Pentateuch (the first five books of the Hebrew Bible). The verb *diaspeirein* occurred more than forty times in the Septuagint, and the noun *diasporá* a dozen times, describing a condition of spiritual anguish and dissolution that accompanied the dispersal of the Jews by an angry God. It was used to translate the Hebrew term *za-avah*, which means "a horror," "trouble," or "an object of trembling." In the words of Deuteronomy 28:25, "The Lord will cause you to be defeated before your enemies; you shall go out against them one way and flee before them seven ways. You shall become an object of horror to all the kingdoms of the earth" (NRSV). The *New Shorter Oxford English Dictionary* cites this passage in support of its primary definition of diaspora, "the dispersion of Jews among the

Gentile nations; all those Jews who lived outside the biblical land of Israel."

The Septuagint distinguished between two closely related concepts that later became conflated in Jewish history, *galut* and diaspora. The Hebrew term *galut* (or *golus*), which connotes banishment or exile, referred at first to the experience of the Babylonian captivity. (The related but distinct term *gola* or *golah* referred more neutrally to the physical or geographical places— initially Babylon—inhabited by the dispersed communities.) The Septuagint translated the negative term *galut* into Greek by a variety of words (most often *apoikia*) whose meaning ranged from migration to captivity. *Diaspeirein*, by contrast, was not used to describe the Babylonian captivity, or any concrete event in human history, but the spiritual dimension of divinely imposed exile, or *za-avah*. Over time, these different concepts appear to have merged into a single idea of diaspora as exile, suffering, and possible redemption (but *galut* retained its negative connotation, while *gola* could have a positive dimension).

Diaspora in this sense was at heart a theological concept. The Jews had sinned by disobeying God's law; their punishment was exile and anguish; their only hope was to repent. The sign of their repentance was obedience to the law, and their potential reward was that God might one day return them to the land of Israel. Resting on a particular theory of human salvation, this conception of diaspora belongs to the branch of theology known as eschatology, which is concerned with the unfolding of history and the ultimate destiny of humankind—in this case, the prospect of return in a spiritual and, possibly, a geographical sense. The Jewish conception—which decisively influenced all others—was therefore forward-looking, anticipating eventual redemption, rather than being a simple lament over exile. Centuries and millennia later, when globally scattered peoples of many different kinds turned to the idea of diaspora to explain their suffering, they adapted the Jewish model to their own purposes.

Caution is obviously needed in applying such a theologically specific concept to other people in other times and places. Diaspora carries particular claims about human suffering, salvation, and the direction of history. In their origins, at least, these claims are culturally particular rather than universal. Simply transposing the Jewish model onto, say, East Asian or South Asian history would be simplistic. The same is true of chronology: a purist might object that any attempt to deploy a single category of diaspora across wide stretches of time is anachronistic. People who use the term "diaspora" today, for example, often do so to make claims about nationalism, race, or the politics of identity that are simply irrelevant to earlier periods of history. But no historian would expect migrants and their descendants in widely different times and places to have used a single, unchanging concept. Nor did they necessarily have to use that word at all in order to make sense of their experience within a framework of exile, connectivity, and return.

Using diaspora to understand migration, then, does not mean that one must remain trapped within the theological confines of the original Jewish model. If that were so, most people would not use the term at all today. Throughout history, migrants of many different kinds have experienced their migration as coercive, made connections with their kinsmen abroad, and dreamed of returning to a homeland. Scholars seeking to explain the experience of these migrants can find in diaspora an analytical framework of broad historical and cultural range. The problem, however, is that if the meaning of diaspora is extended too far, the concept quickly begins to lose coherence.

Expanded meanings

Other than the Jewish case, the Armenian diaspora is probably the best known. Armenia's strategic importance—and its historical misfortune—was that it lay in the path of several successive empires. These included the Persian, Greek, and Roman empires in ancient times, the Byzantine in the medieval era, and the Ottoman and Russian in the modern period. Located at the crossroads of Eurasia in the region between the Black Sea and the Caspian Sea comprising parts of present-day Turkey, Georgia, Azerbaijan, and Iran, Armenia stood little chance of maintaining its territorial integrity. The history of the Irish, the Kurds, and the Sikhs is marked by similar accidents of power and geography.

The successive invasions and occupations of Armenia triggered waves of forced and voluntary migration. By the fifth century CE, Armenians had planted colonies in various parts of the Balkans. In the seventh century, many Armenians were deported to Byzantium and others moved there voluntarily. They prospered in trade and politics over the following several centuries. Since the tenth century, Armenians have had a continuous presence in Venice, Paris, London, and other European cities. Armenian migrants established settlements throughout eastern Europe in the eleventh century, in Palestine and Egypt in the thirteenth, and in Persia in the seventeenth. In the twentieth century, large numbers of Armenians moved to the United States. Today, there are an estimated 7 million people of Armenian extraction globally—3 million of them in the Republic of Armenia and 1.5 million in the United States.

Armenians migrated to an unusual variety of places, but many migrant groups have done that. What, then, is the basis of the special claim to diaspora in this case? Armenians not only migrated on a large and persistent scale, but they also lacked an independent state between the collapse of Cilicia (on the southeast shore of present-day Turkey) in 1375 and the proclamation of the present-day Republic of Armenia in 1991. The Soviet Socialist Republic of Armenia masqueraded as an Armenian homeland from 1921 to 1991, but very few people settled there voluntarily, and most Armenians refused to recognize the state's legitimacy. For more than six centuries, then, Armenians abroad maintained a cherished sense of a homeland, yet they had no place of their own to return to.

Although the origins of the Armenian diaspora stretch back through the millennia, events in the twentieth century had a tragic and decisive influence. In 1894–1896 and again in 1909 the rulers of the Ottoman Empire suppressed an incipient Armenian nationalist movement, killing hundreds of thousands and compelling tens of thousands more to emigrate to neighboring Syria or to the United States. Further suppression of the Armenian minority in 1915–1916 resulted in the deaths of some 1.5 million people, out of a population of only 2 million. Most of the survivors fled to the short-lived Russian Republic of Armenia (1918–1920), to Egypt, Iran, and France, or to Argentina and the United States.

The Armenian genocide assumed an even more tragic layer of significance by association with the Holocaust. All conceptions of diaspora derive from the Jewish model, and the events of the 1940s added a terrible new dimension to the narrative of upheaval, exile, and suffering. Armenians are regarded as one of the paradigmatic diasporas not simply because they scattered widely around the world and lacked a homeland for most of their history, but also because, like the Jews, they experienced genocide in the twentieth century. With genocide as a defining characteristic of the modern Armenian diaspora, the history of Armenian migration as a whole took on a new dimension.

The third most widely recognized diaspora, alongside the Jewish and the Armenian, is the African. Here the defining historical event is slavery. The scale of the African slave trade, and the suffering that accompanied it, is staggering. About 11 million Africans were shipped across the Atlantic Ocean to the Americas from the sixteenth through the nineteenth centuries. The slaves and their descendants in the Atlantic world developed the idea of an African diaspora, drawing heavily on the Jewish model of exile, suffering, return, and a sense of being chosen by God.

Exodus provided the central theme. The nineteenth-century spiritual "Go Down Moses," based on Exodus 7:14–16, sung on the

Southern plantations and later made famous by Paul Robeson and Louis Armstrong, opens with these lines: "When Israel was in Egypt's land: Let my People go / Oppress'd so hard they could not stand, Let my people go / Go down, Moses, / Way down in Egypt's land, / Tell old Pharaoh, / Let my people go." Here, in a powerful cross-identification with Jewish history, Israel represents the African American slaves, Egypt is America, and pharaoh signifies the slave masters. The Exodus story continued to inspire African Americans in the twentieth century, from Zora Neale Hurston to Martin Luther King Jr., but it was not until the 1960s that the word "diaspora" came into widespread currency as a description of African migration. It is now the standard term for describing enslaved Africans and their descendants in the Atlantic world.

Since the 1980s, the term has proliferated to an extraordinary extent in both academic and popular usage, to cover migration of all kinds. The reasons for this new popularity lie in a series of related historical developments. The dismantling of European empires inspired new forms of transnational solidarity, especially among people of African descent. Decolonization also led to the displacement of certain migrant populations in various parts of Asia and Africa. Involuntary migrants classified as refugees received international recognition and protection, bringing global attention to the idea of diaspora. The number of international migrants increased dramatically in recent decades. New forms of technology facilitated faster international travel and communication. And national governments began to reach out in new ways to their overseas populations in search of economic and political support.

These developments help explain not only why the term diaspora has become so popular but also why it is used in such a wide variety of ways. The daily newspapers carry stories on the Afghan, Chinese, Eritrean, Haitian, Iranian, Irish, Indian, Jewish, Mexican, Russian, Somalian, Taiwanese, and Tibetan diasporas, to mention but a small sample. Diaspora is the name of an open-source social networking site that bills itself as an alternative to Facebook. The concept of diaspora is central to the humanities and the social sciences, especially history, political science, sociology, international studies, ethnic studies, and literary criticism. Hundreds of books emerge from the presses each year with the word "diaspora" in their titles.

The field of diaspora studies now has its own special centers and journals. Khachig Tölölyan, a Syrian-born professor of English at Wesleyan University, whose Armenian parents moved to the United States by way of Syria, Lebanon, and Egypt, has edited *Diaspora: A Journal of Transnational Studies* since co-founding it in 1991. The Diasporas Studies Center at the University of Toulouse-Le Mirail began publishing a similar journal, *Diasporas, histoires et sociétés*, in 2005. *Diaspora Studies*, published in New Delhi, focuses on Indian migration, while *South Asian Diaspora*, based in the United Kingdom, covers migration from and within the subcontinent. *Habitus: A Diaspora Journal* compares the Jewish experience with others in an international urban context. And there are many others.

The journal *Diaspora*, in its first twenty years of operation, published articles on virtually every group, theme, and topic imaginable for its subject. The inaugural issue equated diaspora with population dispersal in general and urged that a concept previously confined to the Jewish, Greek, Armenian, and African cases be extended to cover a much wider "semantic domain" that included such terms as immigrant, refugee, guest-worker, exile community, and ethnic community. The journal went on to publish articles featuring Japanese, Irish, Tibetan, Jamaican, Ukrainian, Haitian, Chinese, Indian, and Mexican migrations, among others, along with repeated attempts to define what the concept of diaspora means.

Within five years of publishing the first issue, however, the editor warned that the concept had become too capacious and made a valiant effort to rein it in. One scholar nicely captured this problem in an essay "The Diaspora Diaspora," which argued that the concept has acquired so many different meanings that it has lost coherence. Another made the same point by invoking the sense of decomposition and dissolution inherent in the original Greek, suggesting that the idea of diaspora is in danger of falling apart. If everyone is potentially diasporic, and every migration or ethnic group a diaspora, then how much analytical value can the concept retain?

Definitions

Ironically, much of the confusion about diaspora stems from the very quest to impose a definition. Over the last generation, scholars have produced a bewildering variety of typologies seeking to pin down what diaspora is and what it is not. The most influential of these typologies are so comprehensive that almost every form of migration counts—not just the catastrophic cases (Jewish captivity, African slavery, the Armenian genocide, the Irish famine), but also the migration of merchants, workers, and even colonizers. Trying to fit as many criteria as possible into a single definition can result in incoherence. But choosing some criteria at the expense of others can result in a partial account, in both senses of that word—biased and incomplete. Typologies, in other words, have an in-built tendency to become arbitrary. Who decides what the important criteria are?

Particular problems arise when typologies are used as checklists, with a given group qualifying (or failing to qualify) depending on how many of the stipulated criteria it meets. No single group could satisfy all the criteria in the broadest current typologies. But if one settles for, say, six out of ten criteria, it becomes difficult to compare groups in a meaningful way, as the criteria often belong to different orders of experience. Some definitions emphasize the nature of migration, for example, while others concentrate on the character of the migrant experience abroad.

Given this conceptual confusion, one line of inquiry is to ask not what a diaspora "is" but how the term is used and how it produces meaning. Rather than constructing typologies that run the risk of being arbitrary, partial, or excessively broad, this approach focuses on how new forms of identity and culture are constituted. To capture these new forms, cultural critics use terms such as fragmentation, hybridity, and double consciousness. Diaspora opens up new cultural spaces beyond the boundaries of homeland and hostland. The focus here is not on the process of migration but on the connections migrants form abroad and the kinds of culture they produce.

This approach can be quite powerful, especially when studying literature and other forms of cultural representation. But it has one obvious limitation. It is not possible to analyze diaspora in this way unless people articulate a sensibility and leave evidence in words, images, or material culture. The majority of migrants throughout history were poor and barely literate, and the written evidence that has survived about them was produced for the most part by elites. Attributing a sense of diaspora to entire groups of people on the basis of this sort of evidence has obvious pitfalls. Historians of nationalism, similarly, are aware that they should not attribute a strong nationalist sentiment to all people in a given country based simply on the writings and actions of their self-appointed leaders. That historians of migration should encounter a version of this problem is more than a coincidence. Diaspora, for all its emphasis on identity as historically constructed rather than fixed, can in certain usages result in national history writ large, lumping together people of different character in different places simply because they or their ancestors happen to share a common point of origin.

So this still leaves things in a bit of a muddle. People use diaspora in so many incompatible ways today that one might be tempted to jettison the term altogether. It has become a synonym for population movements in general, not just involuntary migration.

It is also used as a shorthand measure of the number of people from a given country living abroad—an "ethnic group," in the simplest definition of that term. The adjective "diasporic," meanwhile, describes a range of different activities and conditions, from the trauma of exile to political mobilization to cultural creativity. There is no reason why one concept should not embrace several dimensions. But if diaspora cannot be pinned down under a single, fixed definition, leaving its meaning open-ended stretches the concept to the point where it loses utility. When faced with a definitional problem of this kind, it is important to take a stand.

To use diaspora as an explanatory device, it is necessary to make at least some stipulations on the origins and nature of migration and on the types of interconnections migrants and their descendants establish abroad. This approach to diaspora does not entail a rigid typology, a checklist of attributes whereby a given population falls in or out of diasporic status based on how many criteria it meets or fails to meet. Instead, it identifies areas of migration history where diaspora is likely to be a helpful mode of explanation.

Here are the stipulations. Although many migrants travel through networks, diaspora tends to have greater explanatory power when applied to forms of involuntary migration rather than to migration in general. Nonetheless, groups who move voluntarily—the great majority—can engage in diasporic activities abroad, depending on the types of connections they establish. At the most straightforward level, these connections occur when migrants or their descendants in one country continue to involve themselves economically, politically, or culturally in the affairs of their homeland. This connectedness often involves the idea of return to a homeland, sometimes literally but more often metaphorically. The idea of diaspora carries its greatest explanatory power, however, when it involves communication not only between a given overseas community and a homeland but also among various overseas communities of common origin, conceived as nodes in a network or web. In other words, diaspora is most useful when the connections assume a multipolar rather than a unilinear form. The nature of these connections, in turn, carries two corollaries. Diaspora is most relevant when people migrate to several destinations, not just one. And the resulting settlements must persist over time for the kinds of connectivity in question to develop and endure.

Understood in this sense, diaspora has considerable explanatory power. It can illuminate particular aspects of human migration, settlement, and adaptation. But who exactly deploys diaspora for this purpose? Is it an explanatory device used by scholars and other social commentators for analyzing what other people do? Or does it provide meaning to migrants themselves, as they grapple with their own experiences? Put another way, is diaspora a category of analysis or a category of practice? The answer is that it is both. People who write about migration use diaspora as one of their central categories. But actual migrants and their offspring— those who move in certain ways and form particular kinds of connections—also use the idea of diaspora to make sense of their experience, to build communities, to express themselves culturally, and to mobilize politically. Any scholarly conception of diaspora needs to be congruent with the everyday experiences of these people. This point may seem too obvious to be worth making, but some claims about the hybridity and fragmentation of migrant identities raise doubts about whether real people think about their world in quite so tortured a fashion.

The idea of diaspora, then, involves a particular perspective or viewpoint on the world of migration. Phrases such as "the Armenian diaspora in America" or "the Pakistani diaspora in Bradford" are simply shorthand measurements for the number of people from a given location living abroad. In themselves, these phrases explain little. They anchor people firmly in one place, reduce diaspora to a countable entity, and equate it with the term "ethnic group." But the idea of diaspora, in the flexible sense proposed here, can illuminate particular aspects of the world migration creates, revealing a dynamic range of patterns, connections, and interactions. Diaspora enables people to make claims about their world, and this is true of impoverished migrants seeking to make sense of their disrupted lives, nationalist leaders in overseas communities working to build links with their homeland and with their fellow exiles elsewhere, and journalists, professors, or students who write about the subject.

Chapter 2
Migration

When it comes to the process of migration, the term "diaspora" can have two quite contrary implications. Used in one sense, diaspora flattens out social and temporal distinctions, lumping all members of a given migrant group into a single undifferentiated category based on their place of origin. Phrases such as the "Irish diaspora" or the "Italian diaspora" often refer to all people who happened to migrate from Ireland or Italy, along with their descendants, regardless of the circumstances of their migration or the nature of their history abroad. Used in this way, diaspora has a strong tendency to homogenize. Attaching the label "diaspora" to the entire migration of a given group, moreover, can reduce that migration to its single most traumatic form—be it the Babylonian captivity, the Atlantic slave trade, the Irish famine, Indian indentured labor, or the Armenian genocide. Migrations, however, are rarely uniform. People who leave the same place during the same period can do so for radically different reasons. Even during periods of catastrophe and political upheaval, not everyone who leaves is forced to do so. And, above all, the character of every group's migration changes substantially over time. Used in a more critical sense, diaspora is a powerful tool for making just these kinds of distinctions. The idea of diaspora can reveal important variations, not just between migrant groups but also within these groups. Rather than being a simple synonym for migration, diaspora in this sense illuminates particular aspects of migration and the world that migrants create.

Early migrations

Humans have been migrating, as individuals and in groups, for as long as the species has existed. Prehistoric migration, to the extent that we can know about it, is intrinsically fascinating. Yet, in the absence of knowledge about motivations and sentiments, little is gained by calling the migration a diaspora. In this case, the word "migration" will surely suffice. Diaspora is not a neutral or passive term: it carries claims about motivations and feelings. As there is almost no evidence on which to base these claims for the prehistoric period, the term "diaspora" can apply in only the least helpful of ways: scattering or dispersal in a generic sense.

In evolutionary time, *Homo sapiens* emerged very recently, no more than 200,000 years ago. Humans have not physically evolved since, apart from some minor and inherently meaningless variations in skin color, hair, and body shape. According to the latest scientific research, everyone alive today is descended from a small group of anatomically modern humans, *Homo sapiens*, which emerged in East Africa. Recent genetic studies demonstrate that all mitochondria within human cells descend from a single woman, who lived in Africa between 150,000 and 200,000 years ago. This "African Eve" was not the only woman on earth at the time, but mitochondria from no other women have survived. Studies of the male Y chromosome trace the origins of all humans back to the same period. This new genetic research has largely invalidated the older, multiregionalist theory that different varieties of man—the so-called races—evolved from different hominid ancestors. For this theory to be valid, the mitochondrial studies would have to reveal a much wider degree of genetic variety. There is only one type of human.

Homo sapiens did not emerge out of nothing. The species evolved and branched off from earlier hominids. The first bipedal hominids emerged in East Africa about 4 million years ago when a group of apes, now known as *Australopithecus*, began to stand upright. This gave them a significant evolutionary advantage over other apes.

Archaeologists working at Hadar, Ethiopia, in 1974 discovered hundreds of bone pieces, subsequently dated as more than 3 million years old, from the skeleton of an australopith whom they called "Lucy." (A later find in Ethiopia, in 1994, of an earlier protohuman species, was 4.4 million years old.) Protohumans of Lucy's kind moved outward from their point of origin, ranging from Ethiopia as far west as Chad and as far south as South Africa, foraging vegetable matter as they went. They continued to migrate in search, no doubt, of better food and suitable mates.

About 2 million years ago, the genus known as *Homo* branched off from *Australopithecus*, once again in East Africa. They had larger brains than the australopiths and handled tools, made from stones and bones, more deftly. Different varieties of *Homo* and *Australopithecus* co-existed for a long time, but by 1 million years ago the last of the australopiths were gone. The best-known example of the *Homo* genus, *Homo erectus*, was the first hominid to explore and settle the earth outside Africa. As hunter-gatherers who ate meat as well as vegetable matter, the members of this species were mobile by definition. Migration was built into their way of life. Hunter-gatherers needed access to a lot of land to sustain a relatively small group of people, compared with later agricultural or urban societies. When they migrated in large groups, drought and other natural challenges may have been the most common cause; when they did so as individuals or in small groups, the search for mates no doubt also played a part. Beyond that, we cannot know why they migrated or how they felt about doing so.

But we do know from archaeological evidence that *Homo erectus* traveled the earth to an astonishing extent. Fossil remains have been found as far apart as Jordan, the Caucasus, Indonesia, and China. The remains of "Java Man" are estimated to be 1.8 million years old, while those of "Peking Man" are at least 1 million years old. Different varieties of *Homo erectus* evolved outside Africa, and some reached Europe about 500,000 years ago. Neanderthal men—whose remains were first found in Germany's Neander Valley in 1856—probably descended from this group. Neanderthals lived in Europe, and parts of western and central Asia, from roughly 130,000 years ago until their extinction around 30,000 BCE.

Neanderthals were displaced by a new kind of man—*Homo sapiens*. The oldest *Homo sapiens* fossils in Africa date to about the same period as the emergence of Neanderthals. A human skull discovered in Ethiopia in 1967 is about 130,000 years old. Subsequent discoveries indicate the presence of physically modern humans in the region at least 30,000 years before that. Their chief advantage over their predecessors had less to do with brain size or skull shape than with enhanced ability to communicate, probably facilitated by a more flexible larynx. Previous hominids could communicate in rudimentary ways but only modern humans developed language.

Homo sapiens encountered Neanderthals when they moved out of Africa into the Middle East and Europe. The degree of interaction between them is disputed. The standard definition of a species is that it cannot produce viable or fertile offspring with another species. The DNA of modern humans and Neanderthals is almost identical, but a tiny amount differs. Identifying this DNA from fossils is challenging because of the risk of contamination by humans. A study in 2011 suggested that all non-African humans had a small percentage of Neanderthal DNA, which could only have happened through one or several instances of interbreeding. This interaction would probably have occurred during the first encounters in the Middle East. These findings did not revive the multiregionalist theory of human origins, but they unsettled some certainties. The study, if valid, would support the classification of *Homo sapiens sapiens* and *Homo sapiens neanderthalensis* as members of a single hominid species, with modern humans as the last and most successful subgroup. But a counterstudy in 2012 argued that the commonality in DNA simply derived from the fact that the two species at one point had a common ancestor.

Whatever its relationship with its hominid rivals may have been, *Homo sapiens* quickly replaced them and claimed lonely supremacy as the last of its line. Unlike some animals, we have no close relatives: we killed those we once had, or drove them to extinction. *Homo sapiens* went on to populate the earth—first Africa, then Asia and Oceania, and eventually Europe and the Americas. In this intriguing if admittedly very general sense, all of human history is the history of the African diaspora.

Unlike earlier hominids, *Homo sapiens* learned to speak and eventually to read, write, and create art. But literacy and culture emerged late in human history, and without written or visual sources historical knowledge is limited. Much has been learned from archaeology and, more recently, from genetic analysis, but most of the human story will remain forever concealed in the fog of "prehistory." Even history proper, which begins at most 10,000 years ago, is for the most part obscure. Only with the rise of ancient civilizations can one begin to make solid claims about human consciousness. It was in ancient Jewish history that a fully articulated concept of diaspora emerged as an explanation of human migration. It is with Jewish migration, then, that the history of diaspora begins.

Jewish migrations

Diaspora is such a powerful concept that, when used as a shorthand description of Jewish migration as a whole, it can obscure important distinctions. Using diaspora as an all-encompassing term for the history of Jewish migration pays little heed to the actual processes whereby Jewish people moved from place to place, which varied considerably over time. Jewish migration had several discrete phases, which must be distinguished from one another. Many Jewish people were forcibly displaced by wars and persecution, but many others migrated by choice—as soldiers and traders, for example, or in search of family members. Those who settled abroad often decided not to return, even when it was possible to do so. Used in its more critical and analytical sense, diaspora can be a powerful tool for distinguishing between different kinds and phases of migration.

Jewish migration in the ancient world was complex: causation and motivation varied considerably by time and place. Jewish communities flourished throughout the Hellenic world, from Alexandria to Babylon and Sardis. During the era of the Second Temple (515 BCE–70 CE), some Jews left Judah of their own accord and others were driven out by military conquest, as when Alexander the Great invaded in 332 BCE. Return to Israel—an unchosen option in earlier centuries—became impossible after the destruction of the Second Temple in 70 CE. and the razing of Jerusalem in 135 CE. There was no place to which the Jews could return, even if they wanted to do so.

Yet the centuries of dispersal that followed cannot be reduced to a simple story of compulsory migration. Jewish people, to be sure, were repeatedly uprooted by persecution or wholesale deportation. But they also migrated of their own volition, from Palestine or from their new settlements elsewhere, seeking out fellow Jews around the world with whom they could live and prosper as distinct communities. From these patterns of migration, both voluntary and involuntary, emerged the Sephardim and Ashkenazim, the two principal Jewish population groups today. Jews who settled in the Iberian Peninsula came to be known as Sephardim, after the Hebrew word for Spain, *S'farad*. Those who moved through Italy to France and the Rhineland, and from there to Central and Eastern Europe, became known as Ashkenazim, after the Hebrew word for Germany, *Ashk'naz*. Today, the Ashkenazim constitute perhaps 80 percent of all Jews globally.

Regardless of the actual reasons for their migration, most Jews interpreted their life outside Israel theologically. In diaspora they had a concept ready-made for this task. Jews believed their dispersal was God's punishment for disobeying the law as revealed to Moses. This conception of diaspora was largely negative, incorporating the idea of *galut* (physical exile) into the original framework of *za-avah* (spiritual alienation). Diaspora held the promise of redemption, in the form of return, but this was a distant goal that would be of God's making rather than man's.

The early Christians, meanwhile, developed their own concept of diaspora. Seeing themselves as a dispersed pilgrim community spreading the seed of Christ's word until he should return, they were in exile from the heavenly City of God. They agreed with the Jews that Jewish dispersal was God's punishment, but they disagreed with them on the nature of the offense. Christians believed that Jews were destined to wander the earth not because they had disobeyed the law as revealed to Moses, but because they had crucified Jesus instead of recognizing him as the Messiah. For most of the Common Era, hating Jews on these grounds was not just a form of bigotry: it lay at the heart of what it meant to be Christian.

Jewish migration cannot be understood outside this context of intolerance. Some Jews fled in direct response to persecution, others to forestall the possibility. The threat was ever present, eroding any easy distinction between voluntary and involuntary migration. Ashkenazi Jews fled the Rhineland for Poland in the thirteenth and fourteenth centuries to avoid persecution. Sephardim who had converted to Christianity endured torture and execution under the Inquisition until, in 1492, Ferdinand and Isabella decided to expel all of Spain's Jews. Many of these Sephardim settled in Portugal, only to be expelled again within a few years. The Iberian Jews eventually scattered throughout the Mediterranean world as well as the Netherlands and the Americas. The Jews who left Germany for the United States in the mid-nineteenth century did so, for the most part, not to escape persecution but to seek greater economic opportunity and religious tolerance abroad.

But it was anti-Jewish sentiment of the most violent kind, once again, that triggered the great Jewish migrations from Russia in the late nineteenth century. Jews made up less than 5 percent of the population of imperial Russia at this time. More than 90 percent of these Jews were forced to live in a western zone of the Russian empire designated as the Pale of Settlement (comprising parts of present-day Ukraine, Poland, Belarus, Latvia, and Lithuania), created during the reign of Catherine the Great in 1791. By prohibiting permanent Jewish settlement outside this region, the imperial authorities hoped to protect the emerging Russian middle class from business competition. Concentrating the Jews in one region also made them easier targets for violent attack and deportation.

Russian anti-Semitism reached a new peak after 1881, when it was revealed that some of the assassins of Tsar Alexander II were Jewish. Under a series of retaliatory laws, Jews became subject to new prohibitions on settlement, restrictions on property rights, and strict quotas regulating entry into schools and the professions. The assassination also triggered a series of *pogroms*, large-scale mob attacks on Jewish communities that often occurred with the tacit approval of the authorities. The result was an exodus of about 2 million Jews from the Pale of Settlement, first to the Austro-Hungarian Empire and then, via Germany, to the United States. An estimated 75 percent of the world's 7.7 million Jews in 1880 lived in Eastern Europe, and only 3 percent in the United States. Forty years later, almost a quarter of the world's Jews lived in the United States.

The history of Jewish migration, then, cannot be told as a one-dimensional story of involuntary exile, however attractive the simple clarity of that narrative may be. Jewish migration was multifaceted, featuring voluntary as well as involuntary movement and elaborate networks based on family, religion, and business. Yet, because of Christian hostility, Jewish history also unfolded within a unique context of intolerance, hatred, and fear that reached successive peaks in the Inquisition, the expulsion of the Iberian Jews, the Russian pogroms, and the Holocaust. Throughout history, moreover, Jews interpreted their dispersal as a form of divinely imposed exile. The idea of diaspora therefore provides a compelling framework for understanding Jewish migration, provided that due attention is paid to diversity as well as continuity.

African migrations

The same is true of migration by Africans and their descendants. The idea of an African diaspora emerged from the world of Atlantic slavery. Yet, while forcible relocation via the slave trade was by far the most important of the several phases of African migration, the periods before and after the Atlantic slave trade deserve attention too. Despite the centrality of slavery, it is important not to reduce African migration to a single form. And even slavery cannot be approached as an undifferentiated whole. As in the Jewish case, the category of diaspora, when critically deployed, can discriminate between different kinds of population movement, revealing the internal diversity of migration.

Leaving aside the prehistoric migrations of *Homo sapiens*, the first major expansion by Africans was that of the Bantu-speaking people from present-day Nigeria and Cameroon to other parts of Africa and to the Indian Ocean, which began around 3000 BCE. In a second significant wave of migration, from the fifth century BCE on, merchants, soldiers, and slaves began to move out of Africa, forming small communities in Portugal, Spain, Italy, the Middle East, and India. There is no compelling reason to describe these two early waves of migration as diasporas; their form did not differ from other migrations in any significant way. Yet that is precisely the point. Africans migrated around the ancient world in much the same way as other groups. It was only the rise of modern slavery that led to the ahistorical assumption that all African migration must always have been involuntary.

The slave trade, too, varied considerably by time and place. Its best-known form, Atlantic slavery, began in the late fifteenth century and endured for four hundred years, bringing about 11 million slaves to the Americas. Yet Muslim traders had been transporting slaves to North Africa and around the Indian Ocean rim since about 650 CE, a majority of them females who were sold as servants or concubines, but also substantial numbers of male soldiers and household slaves. This so-called Arab slave trade involved an even larger number of Africans than the Atlantic trade, though over a much longer period, enduring in various forms to the end of the nineteenth century.

Relatively little is known about the enslaved Africans who moved northward and eastward rather than across the Atlantic Ocean. The simplest explanation for this lack of knowledge is that the most rigorous forms of historical scholarship on slavery emerged in, and focused their inquiries on, the Atlantic world. But the nature of slavery in the two regions clearly differed. African women

2. The slave market in Zanzibar, one of the centers of the Arab slave trade, as depicted in the *Illustrated London News*, 1872.

and girls tended to disappear into Muslim households, and boys were sometimes castrated. Rates of intermarriage, social mobility, and assimilation, moreover, were much higher than in the Atlantic world. Communities of African descent can certainly be found in the Arab world today, though typically with mixed cultures and ancestry. But, while the lives of captive Africans varied widely from place to place, diaspora is clearly an appropriate framework for all forms of slavery when that institution is considered under the heading of forcible migration as distinct from community formation.

By far the most intensively studied dimension of slavery is the system that arose in the Americas in the sixteenth and seventeenth centuries and endured until the nineteenth. Between 1600 and 1800, about three-quarters of all migrants to the Americas were African slaves. Slavery filled a labor shortage in areas that grew staple crops—sugar, tobacco, rice, coffee, and eventually cotton. The slaves performed a variety of functions, but the majority were used in commercial agriculture and lived on large plantations. This system of slavery emerged first in the sugar-producing Caribbean—Jamaica, Haiti, Cuba, and other islands—and soon spread to the North American mainland, where it solved the labor needs of tobacco planters in the Chesapeake colonies and rice producers in the Carolinas. Planters in these colonies imported their slaves either directly from Africa or from the Caribbean.

Most of the slaves transported across the Atlantic Ocean from Africa went to Brazil or the Caribbean. Brazil was the largest single destination for African slaves, attracting almost 40 percent of those who were shipped across the Atlantic. The Caribbean colonies of the British, French, Spanish, and Dutch empires accounted for another 45 percent. The English colonies on the North American mainland imported only about 6 percent of the total—600,000 to 650,000 Africans—but this relatively small migration eventually gave rise to the largest slave system in the world, based in the Cotton Kingdom of the nineteenth-century South. Slavery in the

United States differed from slavery elsewhere because it became a self-reproducing system. Long before the external slave trade was cut off in 1808, the slave population in the colonies that would later become the United States was growing naturally through an excess of births over deaths. But if slaves within the United States lived longer and had higher levels of material sustenance than their counterparts elsewhere, they also belonged to a closed system from which there was little chance of escape.

Outside the United States, conditions were harsher and slaves were often worked to death. Planters in Cuba and Brazil continued to import slaves from Africa, mainly young men and children, throughout most of the nineteenth century. Males heavily outnumbered females in these countries, and the majority of the slaves were African-born at the time of emancipation in the 1880s. Among slaves in the antebellum American South, by contrast, sex ratios were equal and nearly all the slaves were American-born by the outbreak of the Civil War. Slaves in parts of the Caribbean and South America therefore had more direct connections with Africa than slaves in the United States. But the predominance of males, brutal labor conditions, and higher rates of liberation for those who survived the ordeal all posed serious obstacles to the formation of durable slave communities of the North American kind in the Caribbean and South America.

In African migration, it is the element of compulsion that stands out—more starkly than for any other form of migration. Diaspora is an especially useful category for explaining this form of population movement. The horror of slavery should not obscure the extent of African migration in the ancient world. Nor should it obscure the currents of global African migration since 1900, both by Africans leaving their continent and by people of African origin moving freely throughout the Atlantic world. But slavery was the decisive force. Without the Middle Passage—the ordeal of forced migration from one side of the Atlantic to the other—there would be no

African diaspora. Very little evidence remains from individuals who endured that ordeal, but the descendants of those who survived made sense of their history explicitly within the framework of diaspora. Scholars who seek to reconstruct that history, for that very reason, find considerable explanatory power in the concept.

Irish migrations

In the nineteenth and early twentieth centuries, some 55 million Europeans moved to the Americas. Their epic journey is the best-known episode in the history of global migration. To what extent is diaspora a useful category in this case? The word is frequently applied to European migrants, as in phrases such as "the Scottish diaspora," "the Italian diaspora," or "the Greek diaspora." Yet phrases of this kind tend to use the term generically, either as a substitute for migration or as a measure of the number of people living abroad. Other than indicating that people moved to several destinations in significant numbers, these phrases usually make no specific claims about the origins, form, or character of migration, even if they do often refer to the scale of migration and to particular kinds of sentiments and connections generated abroad. One European migrant group, however, stands out from the others in this respect: the Irish.

Scholars who write about the concept of diaspora tend to exclude European migrants, with the significant exception of the Irish. Those who specialize in Irish migration, for their part, frequently use the word "diaspora," along with related terms such as "exodus" and "exile." Why? The answer lies in three distinctive characteristics of Irish history. Ireland was a British colony for most of the modern era. In the midst of British rule, the country succumbed to the catastrophic famine of 1845–1851, which killed more than 1 million people and scattered more than 2 million around the world, out of a population that reached an all-time peak of 8.5 million just before disaster struck. And for the rest of the nineteenth century, Ireland had the highest emigration rate in

Europe. Because of these three distinctive characteristics, diaspora can be an especially useful mode of explanation in the Irish case.

Yet the tragedy of the famine looms so large that it can obscure the diversity of Irish migration and its changing character over time. The massive wave of migration triggered by the famine makes sense within the framework of diaspora. But the famine migration was only one especially intense episode in a three-hundred-year history of mass migration from Ireland that began around 1700 and has continued with only intermittent breaks ever since. The famine migration has a tendency to overshadow all others. The important thing, once again, is to distinguish between different kinds of migration. And the category of diaspora can be very useful for this purpose.

Since 1700, somewhere between 9 and 10 million people have left Ireland for all destinations. Fewer than 6.5 million people live on the island today (the Republic of Ireland and Northern Ireland combined). By comparison, 35 million Americans list "Irish" as their primary ethnic identity. Most of the Irish who crossed the Atlantic in the eighteenth century were Presbyterians from the northern province of Ulster. They left in pursuit of land, economic opportunity, and religious toleration. From the 1830s to the 1920s, by contrast, Roman Catholics accounted for roughly 90 percent of the transatlantic flow. Almost 1 million people left Ireland for North America in the generation leading up to the famine, due to population expansion, scarce land, and the absence of an urban-industrial infrastructure. In the postfamine era (1855–1921), another 3.5 million left for North America, Australia, and New Zealand, and the exodus continued throughout the twentieth century when the migrant stream was diverted mostly to Britain. Remittances from migrants financed much of the movement out of Ireland.

Diaspora does not seem especially useful or necessary in explaining Irish migration in the 150 years before the famine or the 150 years that followed. The impetus was mainly economic:

3. In *Economic Pressure* (1936), Seán Keating captured the bleak finality of departure, a central theme in Irish culture.

pressure to leave, combined with opportunity abroad. One could say that migration of this kind is, in a sense, involuntary. Yet that would collapse the distinction between migration in general and the particular forms of coerced migration, involving slavery, genocide, famine, and political oppression that the category of diaspora is especially well suited to explain.

The famine, however, is a special case. Diaspora is at its most effective in explaining the singular episode of Irish migration unleashed by that catastrophe. The potato blight, a fungal infestation called *Phytophthora infestans*, was unknown in Europe before 1845. People at the time had no idea what it was. The blight affected much of western Europe, but it spread most rapidly in damp conditions, and nowhere was damper than Ireland. Only in Ireland, moreover, did the population depend so overwhelmingly on the potato. The blight struck repeatedly in the late 1840s, devastating the Irish potato crop. Between 1 and 1.5 million people died of starvation and famine-related diseases. In the ten-year period beginning in 1846, 1.8 million Irish people fled to North America, more than 300,000 settled in Britain, and tens of thousands more moved to Australia.

Popular memory on both sides of the Atlantic—but most enduringly in the United States—long held the famine to be the result of deliberate British negligence or worse. Large sectors of British public, journalistic, and government opinion saw the crop failure as a stroke of providence. God was intervening in history to solve the Irish problem by stamping out laziness, ingratitude, and violence and remaking the country in England's image. "The British account of the matter, is first, a fraud—second, a blasphemy," the Irish nationalist John Mitchel declared from exile in America in 1860, in a book called *The Last Conquest of Ireland (Perhaps)*. "The almighty, indeed, sent the potato blight, but the English created the famine." For Mitchel, the famine was a straightforward matter of genocide, in the sense of deliberate, systematic extermination.

Few historians today would agree with so sweeping a judgment, even if most would argue that the British government could have done more to provide relief. Mitchel was wrong, in a literal sense, but to understand the sentiments of those who actually migrated, his position must be taken seriously. Mitchel gave voice to a belief that became foundational in Irish-American ethnic identity: that emigration was a matter of British-imposed exile rather than voluntary choice. Irish migrants during the famine era had good reason to think of their departure as banishment. Even though they had not literally been banished, many saw themselves as exiles rather than voluntary emigrants. In its definition of diaspora, the

New Shorter Oxford English Dictionary includes as its illustrative example, "the famine, the diaspora and the long hatred of Irish Americans for Britain."

As far as the process of Irish migration is concerned, then, diaspora is a particularly useful category for the famine era. The migration was triggered by a catastrophic event. The migrants scattered to several destinations around the world. And they carried with them a sense of banishment and grievance that became central to their identities abroad. Yet an understanding of history derived from this one tragic era cannot be transposed onto Irish migration as a whole without reducing a complex story to a morality tale. Migrants left Ireland over a period of several hundred years, and they did so for many reasons, not just to escape starvation or British oppression.

Asian migrations

Historians are only beginning to appreciate the full scale and significance of Asian migration in the modern era. Some 30 million people left India for foreign destinations in the century after 1840 and another 20 million left China. In other words, about as many Chinese and Indians migrated in this period as the number of Europeans who settled in the Americas (and these figures do not include an additional 30 million Chinese who moved overland into Manchuria). Why, then, has European migration in the Atlantic world become the model for migration history as a whole? The simplest answer is lack of historical research. But the lack of attention to Asian migrants—especially those who moved within Asia—also rests in part on a long-standing Orientalist assumption that history proper somehow belongs to the West. Asians and Africans, from this perspective, enter history only when they move into the Atlantic world. The best-known Asian migrant groups, consequently, are the bonded laborers from India and China who came to the Americas.

A quick glance at the existing historical literature might suggest that this group of migrants was typical of Asian migration as a whole. Yet they accounted for less than 4 percent of all Indian and Chinese migrants who moved to other countries in the century after 1830. The vast majority of Asian migrants in this period neither migrated to the West nor signed contracts binding their labor to pay off debts incurred in the process of migration. From the perspective of global history, therefore, focusing on Asian bonded laborers in the Western Hemisphere is a gross distortion. Yet, from the perspective of diaspora, this focus has a certain merit. The concept of diaspora offers a way of explaining certain aspects of the migrant experience rather than a general theory of migration. The aspect it explains best in the Asian case is the movement of unfree workers to distant locations. Their migration involved a significant degree of coercion, they endured racism and labor exploitation of an especially harsh kind, and they stayed abroad for long periods or indefinitely.

Considered as a whole, Asian intercountry migration displayed a particular pattern in which short-term movement took precedence. The typical migrant within Asia was a sojourner rather than a permanent settler. Most transatlantic migrants embarked on a single, decisive journey and did not return to Europe. By contrast, only about one-quarter of the Indians who moved to Southeast Asia in the century before World War II stayed there (6 million out of 28 million). Naturally, there are some important exceptions to this rule. Slavic and Italian migrants a century ago, for example, came to America as "birds of passage," intending to go home after a few years, just as many Mexicans and Dominicans do today. And large numbers of Indian and Chinese migrants settled permanently in other Asian countries, eventually forming sizable urban communities. Yet the majority of Asian migrants returned to their home countries after short periods of labor abroad. Many repeated the cycle several times.

Bearing this pattern in mind, diaspora is clearly more relevant to some forms of Asian migration than to others. Migrants who settle permanently in distant places sometimes, but by no means always, form strong connections with their homelands or with people of common origin elsewhere in the world. Seasonal migrant laborers rarely do so, even when their migration involves elaborate transnational networks. Recent scholars have paid considerable attention to these networks—based on family, friends, business, or the state—and the concept of diaspora, with its emphasis on connectivity, is potentially quite useful in this respect. But if one considers Asian migration strictly from the perspective of the degree of freedom involved, diaspora is most relevant when considering the subset of migrant workers who moved under arduous conditions to distant locations from which return was difficult or impossible.

Having considered these migrants thus far under the single heading of "Asian," it is important now to separate the Indian and Chinese cases. Indian labor migration took place within the framework of the British Empire. The workers traveled on British ships to British colonies under the supervision of British colonial officials working in consultation with employers in the receiving locations. In the century after 1840, between 12 and 15 million Indians went to Burma, about 8 million to Ceylon (today's Sri Lanka), and about 4 million to Malaya. The remainder went farther afield, to the islands of the Pacific and Indian oceans, including Fiji, Mauritius, and Réunion; to Kenya, Tanzania, Uganda, and South Africa; and to the Caribbean.

Unable to pay their own way, most Indian migrant workers relied on assistance, redeeming their debt through labor. Relatively small numbers of Indian workers had been migrating to Ceylon and Burma on a seasonal basis for centuries. To finance their passage, they turned to middlemen known as *kangani* who lent money to the migrants or their families. The workers then paid off the debt in installments. With the development of tea plantations in Ceylon, large-scale rice production in Burma, and rubber plantations in Malaya in the second half of the nineteenth century, the *kangani* system supplied the massive demand for Indian labor. Under the *kangani* system, foremen or trusted workers returned from foreign plantations to recruit siblings, kinsmen, and fellow caste-members. Successful *kanganies* established themselves as brokers and merchants in a network that carried millions of Indian workers abroad. The proximity of Ceylon, Malaya, and Burma allowed for a cycle of seasonal labor migration from India characterized by considerable back-and-forth movement. Indians also migrated to Sumatra and other parts of Indonesia to work on tobacco and rubber plantations. These migrant workers typically traveled with return tickets, and about three-quarters of them went back to India.

Those who traveled to more distant locations, by contrast, were generally bound to five-year labor contracts, which they often renewed at the end of their term. In both the Indian and the Chinese cases, indentured migrants came to be known as "coolies," a term that was often extended to cover working-class Asians in general. The etymology is unclear. Possible sources include the Tamil *kuli* (payment for menial labor), the Urdu *quli* (labor or service), the Chinese *ku-li* ("bitter labor"), and the Portuguese name for the *Koli* people of Gujarat. Whatever the derivation, the term was clearly derogatory in British and American usage.

The system of long-distance labor migration, which arose to fill the labor shortage created by the abolition of slavery, was much harsher than the *kangani* system. The workers signed contracts, known as indentures, selling themselves into servitude in return for passage across the ocean, along with food, clothing, and accommodation during their periods of service. Between 1830 and 1916, more than 500,000 Indians traveled to the Caribbean (especially Trinidad, Guyana, Suriname, and Jamaica); about the same number went to Mauritius, another 152,000 to Natal (South Africa), 32,000 to East Africa to work mainly on railroad construction, and 61,000 to Fiji (after its annexation by Britain

4. An Indian worker on a tobacco plantation in Sumatra, Dutch Indonesia, ca. 1900.

in 1874). In sharp contrast to the Asian locations, only one-third of Indian migrant workers returned from Mauritius, about 30 percent from Natal, and 20 percent from Trinidad.

In the Chinese case, as in the Indian, migration to more distant destinations—Hawaii, California, the Caribbean, British Columbia, Peru, and Australia—typically involved indentured labor. This kind of labor was not common for Chinese migrants within Asia, with the significant exception of the tobacco plantations in Sumatra. In all, about 750,000 Chinese migrated as indentured laborers in the nineteenth and early twentieth centuries, moving in roughly equal numbers to Sumatra, the United States, and the Caribbean and Latin America. Like most Asian migrants before the twentieth century, Chinese indentured laborers were heavily male, although a small number of women migrated to work as prostitutes.

The Chinese, like the Indians, developed elaborate systems to finance labor migration. In both cases, this migration existed across a spectrum in which long-distance contract labor was the extreme form. At the least formal end of the spectrum, the Chinese had a version of the *kangani* system whereby individual labor brokers advanced money for the fare and other expenses to families, and migrants paid off the debt with their earnings. Under the "credit ticket" system, a professional labor broker or a shipping company (often acting for a European or American trading house) offered the same arrangement, while retaining tighter control over the migrants during their period of service. The migrants paid off the debt either directly to the brokers or to employers who bought the contract. In its harshest forms, the credit system merged into indentured servitude, with the workers receiving no income until their debt was paid. British control over key ports such as Hong Kong partly determined the composition of population flows, but Chinese migration was not subject to the tight imperial regulation exerted in the Indian case. Networks based on family ties, business associations, or region of origin played a more prominent role.

Asian migration to the Americas and the Caribbean differed significantly from the movement of Europeans across the Atlantic with which it coincided. The Brazilian government, to be sure, imported Italian workers in the late nineteenth century, paying their passage in return for periods of indentured labor. But the British government, eager to populate its settler colonies, subsidized the migration of British and Irish settlers to Canada, South Africa, New Zealand, and Australia. By contrast, Indian and Chinese migrant workers had to pay their own way, through labor. It is not hard to detect the racist underpinning: Asian migrants must be compelled to work, otherwise they would revert to their naturally shiftless state. Similar forms of labor discipline for English servants in the Atlantic world had been abandoned at the end of the seventeenth century, in favor of African slavery. Two hundred years later, Asians were imported into the Americas in a tightly regulated system based on the twin assumptions that they were better suited than Europeans for hard work in hot conditions and that they would not work at all unless forced to do so.

Lack of freedom is the salient characteristic of this form of Asian migration. Kidnapping, coercion, and trickery were widespread. Although imperial officials in India were required to certify that the workers were leaving of their own volition, most migrants had only a partial understanding of what they were entering into. The balance between coercive and voluntary migration in the Chinese case is harder to discern, as it lay concealed within a web of business and kinship associations that outsiders could not readily penetrate, but the degree of exploitation endured by the indentured is scarcely in dispute. Shipboard mortality for Indian and Chinese "coolie" laborers was lower than on Atlantic slave ships, but significantly higher than on vessels taking Europeans to the Americas, due to inadequate supervision, overcrowding, poor sanitation, and lack of food, water, and medical attention. Mortality, malnutrition, and disease remained shockingly high on the plantations where these workers settled. The lack of freedom in this migration process, combined with the abuses endured abroad, means that diaspora is a useful category of analysis.

Approaching migration history from the perspective of diaspora clarifies the distinctions between different forms of migration. But the process of movement is just the beginning of the story. Once migrants settle abroad, they develop new connections among themselves, with their homelands, with their new hostlands, and with people from their background living in other communities abroad. Regardless of the form of migration, a sense of diaspora can emerge from the connections forged in the new communities. A standard approach to migration history concentrates on one-directional flows and connections—the movement of people from one country to another, and the involvement of these people in the affairs of their homeland. The idea of diaspora offers a richer, more multifaceted interpretation of the types of connections migrants and their descendants form abroad. At their most interesting, these connections become multipolar rather than unilinear, uniting scattered communities of common origin in a new global network.

Chapter 3
Connections

Banishment, exile, and alienation are keywords in the vocabulary of diaspora. Some migrant groups, especially Africans, were transported against their will. Others, such as Asian contract workers, endured tight restrictions on their freedom. The great majority of European migrants in the modern era were free, but the Irish developed a powerful sense of banishment and exile. Those groups who endured involuntary migration, or who believed their migration was forced rather than chosen, were also among the most likely to experience discrimination, marginalization, and exclusion in their new host countries, which heightened their sense of exile. The experience of racism, in particular, was critical in generating a sense of diaspora.

Yet the fact remains that migrants settled permanently in their new hostlands. Had they not done so, no strong sense of diaspora could have developed or endured. As the prophet Jeremiah advised the Jews of Babylon, "Build ye houses, and dwell in them; and plant gardens, and eat the fruit of them; . . . And seek the peace of the city whither I have caused you to be carried away captives, and pray unto the LORD for it: for in the peace thereof shall ye have peace" (Jer 29:5–7, KJV). Here lay the origins of a model of diaspora that would allow those in exile to carve out a new life wherever they found themselves. Settling abroad, however, did not mean forgetting the lands from whence migrants came and to which they dreamed they might one day return. Attachment to a common place of origin, real or imagined, lay at the heart of the connections migrants formed abroad—among themselves, with their homelands, and with their fellow diasporans in other parts of the world.

By the rivers of Babylon

The city of Babylon, with its mythical hanging gardens, was one of the glories of the ancient world. Located on the banks of the Euphrates River in present-day Iraq, Babylon is thought to have been the site of the Tower of Babel, itself the source of one of the archetypal diasporas in the generations directly following the Great Flood. The book of Genesis tells the story: "And the LORD said, Behold, the people is one, and they have all one language. . . . Go to, let us go down, and there confound their language, that they may not understand one another's speech. So the LORD scattered them abroad from thence upon the face of all the earth: and they left off to build the city" (Gen 11:6–8, KJV). It was to Babylon that the Jewish leadership was exiled in 586 BCE, following the destruction of the first Temple, an event of decisive significance in Jewish history.

Babylon, as depicted in Hebrew scripture, carried strongly negative connotations. Psalm 137:1–4 conveys the sense of exile and sorrow: "By the rivers of Babylon, there we sat down, yea, we wept, when we remembered Zion. We hanged our harps upon the willows in the midst thereof. For there they that carried us away captive required of us a song; and they that wasted us *required of us* mirth, *saying*, Sing us *one* of the songs of Zion. How shall we sing the LORD's song in a strange land?" Babylon retains the connotation of a magnificent city today. But it also signifies exile, alienation, and despair, not only in Jewish history but also to other groups who have embraced the concept of diaspora. Members of the Rastafari movement, for example, use Babylon as another word for Jamaica or the West, the land of slavery. Babylon, then, is not just a physical place: it is also a condition of alienation and exclusion. That condition was one of the central themes of Jewish history, and diaspora provided the explanatory framework.

Irish migration history was also marked by a strong sense of exile, with the famine of the 1840s casting a very long shadow over that history as a whole. Rightly or wrongly, many Irish migrants in the nineteenth century saw themselves as exiles, a perspective that only heightened their attachment to home. Bigotry and discrimination abroad intensified the sense of grievance. The ability of Irish migrants to speak English no doubt assisted their assimilation, yet they were ridiculed for the way they spoke the language. In Britain, the United States, and Australia, the Irish drew criticism for their poverty, their association with violence, and their Roman Catholicism. This criticism sometimes included derogatory words and images portraying the Irish as inherently inferior, with their supposed outward bestiality taken as a measure of their character and intelligence.

Yet, despite the claims of some recent historians, this anti-Irish prejudice clearly did not amount to racial subjugation of the sort inflicted on African Americans or Asian Americans. Irish migrants could enter the United States freely, move around the country without restrictions, become citizens through naturalization, vote, serve on juries, testify in court, and take legal suits. Nor did the Irish elsewhere experience racism worthy of the name, as distinct from bigotry and snobbery. The global Irish, therefore, are unlikely candidates for membership in some diasporic club of the racially oppressed. But the conditions of their dispersal in the mid-nineteenth century, combined with the prejudice they experienced abroad, clearly gave rise to a powerful and persistent sense of migration as exile.

In the African case, exile was absolute and racism definitive. As a form of coerced migration, the Middle Passage has no parallel in scale or brutality. In seeking to make sense of their ordeal, slaves and their descendants eventually found solace in the Old Testament. In the book of Exodus they discovered an inspiring story of liberation from slavery. The idea of an African diaspora emerged most forcefully in the Caribbean and in North America, rather than the

Spanish- and Portuguese-speaking countries of Latin America. Higher rates of mortality, manumission (the freeing of slaves by their masters), and intermarriage in the latter regions, resulting in distinct patterns of community formation, may partly explain this difference. But it may also have originated in the fact that the Protestant cultures of the English-speaking Caribbean and the United States placed greater emphasis on biblical knowledge, especially the Old Testament, than Catholic cultures did. Francophone Haiti, meanwhile, became a haven for people of African descent in large part because it was the first independent Caribbean republic, achieving its independence from France in 1804.

Because Africans came to be defined as a single black race on the basis of Atlantic slavery, it is easy to assume that they were a single people to begin with. The only evidence in support of this proposition, however, is that all Africans have dark skin, which means the proposition really rests on no evidence at all. The slaves came from several different parts of Africa. They spoke mutually unintelligible languages. They believed in different religions, and they adhered to widely divergent cultural customs and political practices. Europeans and Americans enslaved Africans not because of their skin color but to make money. The concept of race emerged to justify this exploitation, giving social meaning to the inherently meaningless fact of pigmentation. Race was imposed rather than chosen, and it became the defining condition of the African experience abroad. Its ultimate expression was chattel slavery, which reduced humans to a form of property, stripped them of all rights, and sought to obliterate their agency and identity.

It was from this unique experience of alienation that the idea of an African people and an African diaspora eventually emerged. The scholar and activist W. E. B. Du Bois insisted on this point. Through the ordeal of slavery in the Caribbean and the United States, he argued, people began to think for the first time of Africa as one land and of Africans, at home and abroad, as one people. The extent to which Africans who moved to other parts of the world developed similar sentiments and connections is not well known. It is a question for additional research.

Race and exile were twin motifs in the history of Asian workers in the Americas. In the United States, Chinese migrant laborers were repeatedly attacked by Irish and American workers. In 1882 a federal law excluded them from entering the country altogether. Under federal naturalization law, Asian immigrants could not become U.S. citizens until the middle of the twentieth century. Among Hindus, the longing for home was often especially intense. The *Ramayana*, one of the two great epics in the Indian canon, became the central text of the Indian diaspora. The *Ramayana* recounts the journey ("ayana") of Prince Rama (who turns out to be an avatar of the god Vishnu): his exile in the forest, his suffering at the hands of the demon king Ravana, and his preordained triumphal return. The sixteenth-century poet Tulsidas produced a Hindi version of the Sanskrit original, which made the epic widely popular among Indians at home and, eventually, abroad. Migrant workers from Trinidad to Fiji, South Africa to Suriname, and Guyana to Malaysia recited verses from Tulsidas's *Ramayana* in public performances, just as wealthier migrants to Britain and America host readings of the text today.

The *Ramayana* appealed to Hindus abroad for several reasons. The central theme of exile and return, along with the happy ending, had obvious attractions. The story is simple, both in its plot and in its characters, with a clear demarcation between good and evil. It lends itself to the popular, devotional style of Hinduism, rather than the more austere philosophical forms. The *Ramayana*, unlike many ancient religious texts, makes few distinctions based on caste and thus it was popular among rich and poor alike. One of its most beloved characters, Hanuman, is a monkey god rather than a human, reinforcing the irrelevance of the distinctions mortals insist on drawing between themselves. The *Ramayana* is, at heart, a deeply conservative work, emphasizing the concept of *dharma* (duty) in personal relationships, parenthood, marriage, and kingship. In a world disrupted by migration, with family structures in disarray, the *Ramayana* offered a consoling message to homesick Indians all over the world.

The novelist V. S. Naipaul, whose ancestors came to Trinidad as indentured workers, captured this sense of exile in his novel *A House for Mr Biswas* (1961). Every evening the old men would gather on the estate, sitting in the arcade of Hanuman House (named for the monkey god in the *Ramayana*) where much of the novel is set. "It was the time of day for which they lived," Naipaul wrote. "They could not speak English and were not interested in the land where they lived; it was a place where they had come for a short time and stayed longer than they expected. They continually talked of going back to India, but when the opportunity came, many refused, afraid of the unknown, afraid to leave the familiar temporariness." And so, evening after evening, "they came to the arcade of the solid, friendly house, smoked, told stories, and continued to talk of India." The longing to return in this case was only heightened by the knowledge of its impossibility. And yet the old men also found comfort in knowing that they could no longer go back. Like so many migrants before and since, they were at home abroad.

There we sat down

To describe the Jewish diaspora simply as a matter of banishment and exile would be to ignore the flourishing of Jewish culture all over the world. In the midst of adversity, Jews prospered economically and culturally. They did not typically expect, or even want, to return to Palestine. If the "ingathering" of the Jews was eventually to take place, God rather than man would bring it about. In the meantime, Jewish people should prepare for redemption by obeying the commands of the Torah.

Although the destruction of the Temple in 586 BCE was catastrophic, it did not entail the destruction of Jewish culture.

Quite the contrary. Even after some of the exiles returned to Jerusalem to build the Second Temple (completed around 515 BCE), Babylon remained the center of Jewish culture. In the Greek and Roman periods, dispersed Jews who could have returned to Palestine generally chose not to do so. Theological considerations aside, there were sound economic, social, and cultural reasons for this decision. In Greek cities from Alexandria to Sardis, Jews prospered economically, enjoyed political autonomy, and maintained their own synagogues, baths, cemeteries, societies, and schools. Antioch and Damascus, likewise, were important centers of ancient Jewish civilization and learning. When the Romans destroyed the Second Temple in 70 CE, Babylon retained its place as a center of Jewish cultural and intellectual life. The version of the Talmud produced there between the third and sixth centuries CE was the most important compendium of rabbinic wisdom on law, ethics, philosophy, and history.

Jeremiah's injunction, "Build ye houses, and dwell in them," runs as a leitmotif through Jewish history to the present day. In the Middle Ages and the early modern era, Jews throughout the Muslim world and on the Iberian peninsula defined themselves primarily through local affiliation rather than simply lamenting a lost homeland in Palestine. The so-called assimilated Jews in nineteenth-century Germany enjoyed a remarkable degree of social and cultural integration. The 3 million or more Russian and eastern European Jews who settled in the United States in the half century after 1880 went there intending to stay permanently. They had no desire to return to Russia nor to join the small number of Jews who were settling in Palestine by that time. Like Jewish migrants before and since, they adapted in varying degrees to local conditions while remaining Jewish.

The Irish, although they encountered considerable initial hostility, also built a vibrant new ethnic culture, especially in the United States. Like Jewish immigrants, Irish Americans tended to have relatively equal sex ratios, which helped foster community formation—in contrast to the often heavily male immigrants from eastern and southern Europe. Despite continuing bigotry and prejudice, they made significant economic advances and gained considerable political power, especially at the city level, within a few generations of the famine. By insisting on their right to retain Catholicism, moreover, the American Irish expanded the limits of cultural pluralism. They would become American but, as far as possible, on their own terms. Subsequent immigrants benefited from this redefinition of assimilation as a reciprocal rather than a one-way or coercive process.

Yet, for all their social and political success, many Irish Americans retained a powerful sense of grievance, blaming all of Ireland's woes on Britain, especially the continued mass migration from the island. Along with Jewish immigrants, the Irish had the lowest levels of return migration from the United States. Although they had a clearly defined geographical sense of home—unlike Jews and Africans—they did not go back to Ireland, even for short visits, when they clearly could have afforded to. Doing so might have undermined the sense of exile at the heart of their ethnic culture. The American Irish were content to settle where they were.

People of African descent, meanwhile, had no choice but to settle permanently in the Americas. Forcibly uprooted and cut off from their native lands, they built new cultures on American soil. The nature of these cultures, and the extent to which African influences survived, depended on the slaves' region of origin, the recency of their arrival, and the ratio of blacks to whites in their new locations. Different parts of the Americas imported slaves from different parts of Africa. These African regions had distinct languages, economies, and political forms. Scholars with a mastery of African as well as American history have traced the resulting cultural diversity from one side of the Atlantic to the other. In all, about 35 percent of the slaves who crossed the Atlantic came from West Central Africa (the states of Angola and Kongo), and another 50 percent from three regions along the West African Coast (the Bight of Benin, the Bight of Biafra, and the Gold Coast). West Central Africans dominated the traffic to Saint Domingue and South America, accounting for three-quarters of those who went to Brazil. Jamaica, by contrast, drew heavily on the Bight of Biafra (southeastern Nigeria) and the Gold Coast. Slaves from each of the four main regions had different languages, cultures, agricultural practices, technologies, and political structures. It was the ordeal of slavery, and the imposition of race, that eventually produced a sense of a common African origin, a people united in diaspora.

The abolition of slavery in the British Empire created a severe labor shortage on the plantations. Planters in Mauritius and the Caribbean, working in close cooperation with British imperial officials, imported Indian workers to meet this demand. A law passed by the British Parliament in 1833 provided for the emancipation of slaves throughout the empire, but only children below the age of six and a half were freed immediately. In an effort to keep the plantation labor force intact, all slaves above that age were bound to a six-year "apprenticeship," during which they were required to perform forty hours a week of unpaid labor for their masters. To further protect the plantation economies, the British government paid the slave owners £20 million in compensation for their loss of property (a massive sum, but only half the estimated capital value of the slaves). Neither measure worked. Investment in the sugar plantations dried up because of fears that production without slavery would be unprofitable. Complete emancipation came in the British Caribbean and Mauritius in 1838, earlier than originally planned. Freed from the constraints of the apprenticeship system, the former slaves quickly abandoned the plantations, leaving the sugar canes to rot. But the planters were already turning to Asian workers as an alternative source of labor.

Conditions for indentured Asian migrant workers were brutal. The workers were housed in the old slave quarters, known in Mauritius as the *Camps des Noirs* and in British Guiana as "the

Nigger Yards." In Mauritius and the Caribbean, they raised staple crops, chiefly sugar, which had been the mainstay of the old slave economy. In Cuba, indentured Chinese laborers worked alongside slaves and were processed through the *Deposito de Cimarrones*, a holding center for runaway slaves. The plantation masters were former or current slave owners, assisted by foremen and estate managers, usually of Asian origin, who brutally enforced discipline. Workers were beaten and sometimes tortured. Sanitary and safety conditions were abysmal. Work-related injuries, malnutrition, vitamin deficiency, hookworm, malaria, and other diseases were common. In the guano mines of Peru, Chinese workers endured some of the most hideous conditions anywhere in the Americas, excavating the accumulated excrement of seabirds for use as fertilizer. Everywhere Asian contract migrants settled— from Fiji to Natal, Cuba to Peru, and Mauritius to Trinidad— suicide rates were alarmingly high.

For Hindus, transportation overseas was especially disruptive of religious and social conventions. Hindu deities, holy places, modes of worship, and dietary practices were often intimately connected to place. The process of relocation and settlement outside India ruptured these connections. The uncomfortable proximity of migrants from different backgrounds, both on the ships and in the plantation barracks, intensified fears about loss of caste through social pollution, especially the sharing of food and water. To address this problem, recruiters drew heavily at first on tribal people, such as the Dhangars, who lived outside the Hindu caste system. During the period of Indian indentured migration as a whole, migrant workers probably came in roughly equal numbers from the lower castes, the agricultural castes, and the artisanal or high castes (with more lower-caste migrants coming from South India, where they made up a higher proportion of the population).

Transported abroad, Indians had no choice but to intermingle, both on the ships that carried them and on the plantations where they settled. Caste distinctions survived but in weakened form.

The imperial labor regime sought to impose uniformity on all Indian migrant workers, regardless of background or location. One indication of the power and efficiency of this regime was that all workers, from the Caribbean to Mauritius and Fiji, were assigned identical rations of tea, rice or bread, and lentils or vegetables.

Life on the plantations wreaked havoc on families. Traditional forms of privacy were impossible, and the preponderance of men over women undermined the institution of marriage. Monogamous relationships gave way to informal arrangements whereby women serviced multiple partners, and men sometimes hired out their wives and daughters. Predictably, the result was considerable jealousy, insecurity, and suspicion, resulting in violence against women, including many murders. In the period after indenture, the descendants of Asian migrant workers took pains to restore traditional family structures, in a patriarchal form that continued to impose severe restrictions on women's choices concerning education, work, and marriage.

The predominantly temporary character of migration within Asia, meanwhile, should not conceal the fact that the Indians and Chinese built permanent communities there, as well as in the Americas. In distant locations outside Asia, such as Trinidad, Fiji, and Dutch Guiana (today's Suriname), people of Indian origin constituted one-third or more of the population by the early twentieth century. In British Guiana, Mauritius, and Réunion they became the majority. These populations numbered in the tens or hundreds of thousands, depending on the location. But in Asia, even though the proportion of migrants who settled permanently was much lower, the gross number of settlers was considerably higher, simply because most Asian migrants moved within rather than beyond the continent. About 1 million Indians lived in Burma in 1931, for example, whose capital, Rangoon, had an Indian majority. In Malaysia in 1947, the almost 3 million Chinese and 600,000 Indians together made up half the population.

Chinese migrants established sizable overseas settlements throughout Asia. In the 1850s, half of all Chinese migrants had settled outside the continent, but from the 1880s through the 1930s, after restrictions were imposed in the United States and Australia, nearly all Chinese migrants moved within Asia. Deploying their own migrant networks, the 20 million Chinese who migrated in the century before World War II settled most heavily in Singapore, Malaya, Thailand, Indonesia, Indochina, and the Philippines. Long-settled ethnic Chinese elites dominated their communities in these locations. About 3 million people of Chinese descent lived in Indonesia in 1947 and 1 million in both Indochina and Thailand. Smaller urban communities emerged on the West Coast of the United States, in New York City, and in Peru and Mexico.

The circuits through which Asian migrants traveled were part of a larger network made up of workers, employers, state officials, merchants, shipping companies, lodging houses, and remittance agencies that sent money back to the homeland. For Indian workers,

5. "The foreign element in New York—the Chinese colony, Mott Street," published in *Harper's Weekly*, 1896.

the British imperial framework provided the essential context, with merchants and middlemen playing an important intermediary role. Tamil-speaking members of the merchant-banking Chettiar caste based in Southeast Asia, for example, financed Indian migration throughout that region, lending money to local employers who could not get ready credit from European banks. Chinese networks based on family, kinship, dialect, and region provided information on work and housing, as well as funding for the passage. The Chinese government, meanwhile, began to forge ties with overseas Chinese communities from the late nineteenth century on, seeking their financial and political support for the homeland—a form of outreach that would assume major dimensions in both Chinese and Indian history in the twentieth century.

When we remembered Zion

Every idea of diaspora involves connection with a homeland, whether real or imagined. This land is often the state or nation that migrants or their ancestors left behind. But people can also develop an intense attachment to the idea of a homeland precisely because they do not have one. Diaspora is a wellspring of nationalism, with migrant communities devoting much of their energy to supporting their homeland, liberating it from foreign rule, or creating an independent nation-state. This sort of political and cultural activism, in turn, can generate connections with people of common origin in other parts of the world.

In the absence of a Jewish state for almost two millennia, nearly all Jewish people lived without a single homeland. For this very reason, their sense of diaspora cannot have been unremittingly negative. Jews defined themselves as a unique people while seeking, in the absence of a single homeland, to live normal lives in the many different countries where they settled. Just as Babylon became a center of Jewish learning in the ancient period, Spain and Portugal before the Inquisition were the sites of a golden age in Jewish culture, marked by philosophical and artistic creativity rather than longing for return. Many Jews in central and eastern Europe during the modern era, likewise, celebrated the creative dimension of diaspora rather than simply lamenting their exile. The extraordinary accomplishments of Jews in the United States are only the latest example, albeit on an unprecedented scale, of a diasporic culture flourishing while rooted in a particular place.

Like the Jews, the American Irish had remarkably low rates of return migration. This pattern of settlement sustained a pervasive belief that the ongoing departure of millions of Irish people overseas was due solely to British colonial oppression. Irish nationalism took various forms: moderates wanted gradual, peaceful change within the existing constitutional framework of the British Empire; republicans demanded immediate independence, achieved through armed force if necessary; a radical minority pressed for fundamental social as well as political reform. Because of the scale of nineteenth-century Irish global migration, these distinct but sometimes overlapping forms of nationalism extended across a network that included Britain, North America, and Australia as well as Ireland. Nationalist leaders such as Charles Stewart Parnell and Éamon de Valera toured the United States to raise funds and enlist political support for an Irish republic. New York City became the leading center of Irish republican activism in the world. Irish nationalists in the United States orchestrated the escape of Irish political prisoners from Australia and planned bombing campaigns in English cities. Nationalist leaders, journalists, and literary figures in Boston, London, Sydney, and Dublin engaged in an ongoing international conversation on the nature of Irish freedom.

This "diasporic nationalism," far from being focused solely on the homeland, provided a means of social and political advancement in the hostland. Irish nationalists abroad were certainly fighting for an independent Ireland, but they were also fighting, in more concrete terms, for acceptance and success in their adopted countries. An independent Ireland, they believed, would raise their status, whether as Americans or as Australians. And the very act of organizing in pursuit of nationalist goals would demonstrate to their critics their growing political acumen and their fitness for citizenship in their adopted lands.

The same was true in the Indian and Chinese cases. Asian nationalist leaders at home and abroad believed that the degraded status of "coolie" laborers reflected poorly on the international reputation of their countries. When Chinese merchants in Shanghai organized a boycott of American goods in 1905–1906, protesting the poor treatment of their countrymen in California, the movement soon spread to Chinese communities in other port cities in Southeast Asia. Political mobilization in India against the abuse of migrant workers within the British Empire led to the gradual abolition of the indentured labor system between 1910 and 1917. Nationalist movements in both India and China in the twentieth century relied heavily on overseas support.

People of African descent, because they were cut off entirely from their places of origin, produced some of the richest cultural and political expressions on the theme of a lost homeland. The very idea of Africa emerged abroad: it had no meaning for slaves transported from their individual regions, states, or villages. Olaudah Equiano, who lived and traveled as a slave and a freeman all over the Atlantic world—from the United States and the Caribbean to England, France, Spain, and Portugal—recounted in his autobiographical narrative in 1789 how his sense of self developed, through the awful experience of slavery, from a form of local affiliation with the region of Africa where he claimed to have been born, to a self-consciously African and Atlantic diasporic identity. He came to see this sense of Africanness, infused by Christianity, as the salvation of his people.

These early attempts to make sense of the African dispersal within the framework of diaspora often cited Psalm 68:31: "Princes shall come out of Egypt; Ethiopia shall soon stretch out her hands unto

God." The verse was sufficiently vague to suggest several meanings. For Ethiopian Christians and, later, members of the Rastafari movement, it signified the transfer of the Ark of the Covenant— the chest, described in the book of Exodus, holding the stone tablets on which the Ten Commandments were inscribed—from Jerusalem to Ethiopia, and the providential mission that came with this transfer. Edward Blyden, a native of St. Thomas in the Danish West Indies who frequently took Psalm 68:31 as his text, emphasized the importance of the African dispersal in world history and argued for the centrality of the idea of Africa to those in exile. After being denied admission to theological colleges in the United States on racial grounds, Blyden moved to Liberia in 1850 and became that country's most prominent diplomat. Other black leaders in the nineteenth century cited Psalm 68:31 as a portent of the coming economic, political, and cultural revival of Africa, hastened by the return of former slaves from the Americas with their Christian religion. Africa, in this view, had gone into decline as a result of not embracing Christianity. A revived Christian African civilization would go on to redeem and rule the world.

Some lesser-known early figures occasionally used the word (and not just the concept) "diaspora" to describe the Atlantic slave trade. Charles Victor Roman in *American Civilization and the Negro* (1916), for example, referred to the Middle Passage as a diaspora. Other commentators described the "Great Migration" of African Americans, which began at the turn of the twentieth century and persisted through World War II, as an exodus from the Egypt of the South to the Promised Land of the North. Not until the 1950s and 1960s, however, did diaspora come into widespread use in the African case. It emerged mainly in the United States and the Anglophone Caribbean and did so under propitious circumstances.

Even as Africa and the Caribbean moved toward decolonization, Jim Crow segregation, lynching, and disfranchisement persisted in the American South. With the United States presenting itself as a beacon of freedom to a world threatened by Soviet tyranny,

American policies on race became an embarrassing liability. Massive agitation from below, in the form of the civil rights movement, resulted in legislation in the mid-1960s overturning the Jim Crow system and securing voting rights for African Americans. Martin Luther King Jr. and other leaders of the civil rights movement saw African Americans as a chosen people whose suffering could redeem the United States as a whole.

With black people engaging in interconnected struggles against racism and colonialism on several fronts—in Africa, the Caribbean, and the United States—diaspora emerged as a powerful unifying theme. The concept provided activists, scholars, writers, and artists with a compelling narrative: captivity in Africa, transportation via the Middle Passage, hereditary slavery in the Americas, and the possibility of eventual redemption. It also offered a framework in which to examine how the slaves remembered Africa; how they and their descendants eventually forged connections with other people of African descent, both locally and globally; and how they might return, literally or figuratively, to their ancestors' homeland.

Songs of Zion

Long before intellectuals began to use the word "diaspora" to explain African global history, slaves and their descendants had been remembering and imagining Africa in a wide variety of cultural forms. Perhaps the most poignant belief among the slaves was that suicides took wing and flew back home to Africa. African-born conjurers and magicians exercised considerable cultural authority on the plantations, sometimes over whites as well as blacks. Many of the songs on the slave plantations were of African origin, not just in their language or content but also in their form. The musical pattern known as "call-and-response" is a classic example. In this style of music, different musicians play or sing distinct phrases, with the second phrase commenting on or responding to the first. The pattern is found today in various forms in jazz, rhythm and blues, and reggae. Typical of many sub-Saharan African countries, call-and-response came to the Americas with the slaves. They used it while singing in the fields, but also—or so their masters feared—to transmit secret messages. Call-and-response was also central to the slaves' religious rituals, even after widespread conversion to Christianity in the nineteenth century. Also of African origin was the counterclockwise ring shout, combining dance and song, found in slave communities throughout the Atlantic world. And African influences were evident in slaves' folk art, from textile designs to quilting patterns, woodcarving, and basket weaving.

Slave religion involved a fusion of African and Western forms. Slaves in the nineteenth century derived much of their theology from non-African sources—the Roman Catholic Church in Latin America or various forms of Protestantism in the United States—but they infused their Christianity with African ideas and rituals. That an individual could be possessed by the Holy Spirit, for example, was consistent with African notions of possession. Scholars have identified particular forms of ecstatic response to the divine—dancing, shouting, shaking, jerking, and fainting—as rooted in African practices.

In the English-speaking Caribbean, Christian slaves deployed supernatural powers both to inflict harm (*obeah*) and to counteract witchcraft and other forms of evil. The religious practices of *convince* and *kumina*, involving worship of ancestors as well as sky gods, had room for a Christian deity among others. *Vodun* (or *voodoo*) traditions of herbal healing and intercession against evil were common in the lower Mississippi region as well as in Haiti. In Brazil, African religious traditions known collectively as *candomblé* were organized by ethnic or national communities (*naçòes*). African-infused forms of Christianity also survived in Cuba (*santería*) and Trinidad (*shango*).

An African dimension of a different sort is evident in the more formal institutional structures of American Protestantism.

During the American Revolution, black southerners organized African Baptist congregations in both Williamsburg, Virginia, and Savannah, Georgia. In 1792 black parishioners walked out of a Methodist Church in Philadelphia after being directed toward segregated seating and formed their own separate congregation. Under the leadership of Richard Allen and Absalom Jones, the Philadelphians formed the Bethel African Methodist Episcopal Church (AME) in 1794. The name "African" in these cases might be dismissed as a synonym for black, used merely for purposes of variation, but the AME leaders strongly supported the efforts of Paul Cuffe, a wealthy African American Quaker sea captain and merchant in Massachusetts, to encourage black migration from America to Africa. Bringing Christianity and commerce to Africa by planting a black American colony there, Cuffe believed, could liberate people on both sides of the Atlantic and restore the fractured unity of the African people.

In the twentieth century, powerful new ideas about African unity and solidarity emerged. These ideas, which often go by the shorthand name of Pan-Africanism, had several disparate strands: W. E. B. Du Bois, who was born in Massachusetts in 1868, stood at the intellectual vanguard of a movement to liberate African Americans—and all people of African descent—through a combination of historical analysis, social criticism, and political activism. A co-founder of the National Association for the Advancement of Colored People (NAACP) in 1909, Du Bois helped organize Pan-African conferences in Paris in 1919, London in 1921, New York City in 1927, and Manchester in 1945. Disillusioned with developments in the United States, he eventually renounced his American citizenship and relocated to Ghana, where he died on August 27, 1963, the day before the March on Washington.

Marcus Garvey shared some of Du Bois's goals, but the two men could not have been more different in temperament and strategy. Born in Jamaica in 1887, Garvey spent some time in London before founding the United Negro Improvement Association (UNIA) in

Jamaica in 1912. He moved to the United States in 1916 and set up the UNIA headquarters in Harlem. The movement for African self-government, Garvey insisted, was every bit as serious as the contemporary global nationalist movement to liberate Ireland or the Zionist movement to reclaim Palestine. The red, black, and green flag he designed—signifying the blood shared by all Africans and shed by them under slavery, the color of their skin, and the natural abundance of their continent—became the emblem of Pan-Africanism, black nationalism, and (along with gold) the Rastafari movement. Garvey's Black Star Line promoted trade between black communities throughout the Americas. His newspaper, the *Negro World*, the most widely circulated of all black publications, appeared in French, Spanish, and Portuguese translations as well as in English. At its peak, the UNIA claimed one thousand branches in forty-three countries.

Pan-Africanism also had a distinctively French literary form known as *Négritude*. This movement emerged among African and Caribbean students and intellectuals living in Paris before World War II. The poet Léopold Senghor, who later became the first president of Senegal, played an important role, along with his fellow poets Aimé Césaire of Martinique and Léon Damas of French Guiana. Alioune Diop, another Senegalese, founded the review *Présence Africaine* in 1947, and writers such as Jacques Roumain of Haiti, Paul Niger of Guadaloupe, and later Édouard Glissant of Martinique established their reputations in its pages. The editors of *Présence Africaine* organized the First Congress of Negro Writers and Artists in Paris in 1956, followed by a second conference in Rome in 1959.

Négritude had several strands. Some proponents of the philosophy, notably Césaire, argued that it was the shared experience of oppression that had created a common African identity. Others, such as Senghor, tended toward the belief that people of African descent had an inner racial essence that distinguished them from non-Africans and found expression in cultural works.

Africans, in this view, were naturally sensual, creative, peaceful, and harmonious. Although this essentialist approach to race was empowering in the context of decolonization, at its crudest it could amount to a form of racial mysticism. The psychiatrist and anticolonial activist Frantz Fanon, probably the first Francophone intellectual to use the term "diaspora" (*la dispersion*), was aware of this dilemma. A student and protégé of Aimé Césaire, Fanon was nonetheless critical of *Négritude*. In his most influential work, *Les damnés de la terre* [*The Wretched of the Earth*] (1961), Fanon advised Africans worldwide to draw strength from the idea of diaspora while rooting themselves simultaneously in their national cultures. Only in that way, he believed, could they be politically effective and psychologically whole. Like Jeremiah's Jews in Babylon, they must seek to prosper in their new lands while remembering Zion. In some cases, that process inspired a literal return to a lost homeland, but for the most part return was more imagined than real.

Chapter 4
Return

Nearly every conception of diaspora features the idea of return
to a homeland in some form. Many migrant groups, such as
the Armenians, did not originate in well-defined homelands.
Yet precisely because they had no concrete place to return to,
they cherished the idea of a homeland all the more, devoting
much of their activity abroad to achieving a nation-state for
their people. But when homelands in the form of nation-states
did eventually become available, people did not simply uproot
themselves en masse from their globally scattered communities.
The great majority stayed where they were. Despite their
well-known sense of exile, for example, very few Irish returned
to Ireland, except during the short-lived decade of economic
prosperity known as the "Celtic Tiger" that began in the mid-
1990s. Nor did the idea of a metaphorical "return" to Ireland
assume spiritual or political dimensions comparable to those
in the African case. Among people of African origin, the dream
of return sustained a sense of diaspora even when physical
relocation was impossible or undesirable. Africa was always
more of an imagined homeland than a concrete geographical
location or a realistic place of refuge. Tens of thousands of
people did move to Africa from the Americas in the nineteenth
century, but even when physical return was out of the question,
the idea of return inspired powerful bonds of solidarity
among people of African descent around the world. As for

large-scale physical relocation to an ancestral homeland, the most significant example was the Zionist movement, which gave rise to the state of Israel.

Zionism

Zionism can be understood, in the historical context from which it emerged, as a form of European nationalism. It rested on the belief that no nation could be complete without expression in the form of a territorially bounded state. The Zionist movement arose in response to the persecution of the Jews in Russia and eastern Europe at the end of the nineteenth century. In *The Jewish State* (1896), Theodor Herzl called for the establishment of a Jewish national homeland in Palestine, where the ancient kingdoms of Israel and Judah had once stood. The first Zionist Congress, held in Basel in 1897, established a national assembly (the World Zionist Organization) dedicated to the creation of a homeland for the Jewish people. The Zionists debated, but eventually declined, a British offer to reserve part of Uganda for this purpose. To survive and prosper as a people, they insisted, the Jews must return to Zion—a symbol for Jerusalem referring to both the biblical fortress and the hill overlooking the city. The Zionist movement sought to create a Jewish state through migration to Palestine, at the time a province of the Ottoman Empire. In a phrase made popular by the Anglo-American Zionist Israel Zangwill in New York City, Palestine was "a land without people for a people without a land." This formulation, however, ignored the fact that at the onset of Jewish migration in the 1880s, Palestine was populated by some 400,000 Arabs and 43,000 Christians (along with about 15,000 Jews).

To describe the successive migrations to Palestine, the Zionists used the Hebrew word *aliyah* (plural *aliyot*), which means "ascent." This word also describes the act of going up to read from the Torah in the synagogue. In migration history, it came to signify the return of the Jews from exile. A Jew who migrated to Palestine (an *oleh*; plural *olim*—both derived from *aliyah*) was ascending, returning to the Promised Land. During World War I, the British supported Arab revolts against the Ottoman Empire, pledging at least tacit support for postwar independence. In the Balfour Declaration of 1917, however, the British government committed itself to the establishment of "a national home" for the Jewish people in Palestine. The commitment took the form of a letter by the foreign secretary, Arthur Balfour, to Baron Walter Rothschild, published in the *Times* of London. Rothschild, a member of one of the most influential international Jewish families, was asked to convey the message to the leaders of the Zionist movement.

British motivation in issuing the Balfour Declaration was and remains controversial. By supporting a Jewish state, Britain could claim to be subscribing to the principle of national self-determination advocated by its wartime ally, the United States. More importantly, a Jewish homeland in the Middle East might protect the route to India, safeguard British interests on the Suez Canal, and act as a buffer between British and French zones of influence. Quite what was meant by "a national home" in Palestine—all of that region, or part of it—was left deliberately vague. And the declaration's casual assertion that this homeland would "not prejudice the civil and religious rights of existing non-Jewish communities" has bedeviled the politics of the region ever since. From the perspective of the existing Arab population, any attempt to set up a Jewish state within Palestine was a form of colonization that could only lead to displacement.

Zionism was a minority movement among European Jews. In its origins and development, the movement was primarily secular, an expression of Jewish nationalism rather than Judaism. From a theological perspective, only providence could bring about the "ingathering" of the Jews; physical return before the arrival of the Messiah was both undesirable and impossible. Of those Jews who fled Russia and eastern Europe between the onset of the pogroms and the outbreak of World War I, the great majority went to the United States, while only about 3 percent chose Palestine. The proportion going to Palestine rose significantly in the 1920s and 1930s, as a result of the combined effect of intensified persecution in Europe and immigration restriction in the United States, but it still did not exceed 30 percent.

In the first *aliyah*, between 1881 and 1891 (before the formation of the Zionist movement), as many as 30,000 Jews left Russia, Poland, and Romania for Palestine. Most of these migrants settled in cities and villages, but a minority established agricultural settlements. They were rescued from failure by the Paris branch of the Rothschild family, which introduced plantation-based agriculture—mainly vineyards—using Arab labor. In the second *aliyah*, from 1904 to 1914, about 40,000 Jews migrated to Palestine, mostly from Russia. Settling on land purchased by the Jewish National Fund, a branch of the World Zionist Organization, these migrants established *kibbutzim* (communal farming settlements) under socialist and cooperative guidelines. They also revived the Hebrew language and founded political parties, trade unions, and newspapers, laying the groundwork for a Jewish state.

The third, fourth, and fifth *aliyot* took place during the period when the British governed Palestine as a Mandate of the League of Nations (1922–1948). The third *aliyah* (1919–1923) consisted of between 30,000 and 40,000 migrants, mainly from Russia and eastern Europe. This wave included many professionals, tradesmen, artisans, and workers with socialist ideals, as well as agronomists and skilled farmers who established a durable economy. The fourth *aliyah* (1924–1929) consisted of 82,000 largely middle-class migrants, threatened by economic ruin in Russia or by anti-Semitism in Poland. The majority did not subscribe to socialist or cooperative principles, and they settled heavily in towns and cities. Some 23,000 of these *olim* subsequently left Palestine for the United States and other locations. But among those who stayed was Vladimir Jabotinsky, the architect of Revisionist Zionism, a militant ideology of self-defense against all enemies of the Jewish people. His underground militia, the *Irgun*, waged a campaign of terror against local Arabs. Blaming the suffering of the Jewish people not simply on anti-Semitism but on the condition of diaspora, which he equated with statelessness, Jabotinsky saw the formation of a secure Jewish state in Palestine as the only answer.

As pressure to leave Europe intensified in the 1930s, the flight of the Jews to Palestine assumed mass proportions. Between 1929 and 1939, some 250,000 *olim*, many of them fleeing Nazi persecution, arrived in Palestine, making up the fifth *aliyah*. They included large numbers of professionals, industrialists, academics, artists, and architects. As Jewish agencies continued to purchase land for settlers, Arab tenants were evicted and displaced. With Arab resentment against the Jewish settlers mounting, the British government placed strict limits on Jewish immigration to Palestine in 1939, hoping to halt the flow altogether within five years. Jewish aid associations resisted this ban throughout World War II, smuggling as many as 111,000 migrants past the British naval blockade or overland via Syria. This was a significant number but only a tiny fraction of those who might otherwise have escaped the Holocaust.

In 1947 the United Nations approved a partition plan dividing Palestine into two states, one for the Jews and one for the Arabs. On May 14, 1948 (Iyar 5, 5708 in the Hebrew calendar), David Ben-Gurion, the executive head of the World Zionist Organization, declared the establishment of the state of Israel. On the wall behind the podium as he read the declaration was a huge portrait of Theodore Herzl, flanked by two flags bearing the Star of David. The new state adopted a highly evocative official emblem: the menorah captured by the Romans in 70 CE, a symbol of the lost Temple in Jerusalem, depicted on the Arch of Titus. The Israeli Declaration of Independence proclaimed *Eretz Israel* (the Land of Israel, or Palestine) "the birthplace of the Jewish people." There the Jews had established their first state and now, after almost two millennia, they were renewing their statehood. "After being forcibly exiled from their land," the declaration stated, "the people

6. Standing beneath a portrait of Zionist leader Theodor Herzl, David Ben-Gurion reads the Declaration of the Establishment of the State of Israel to the Jewish People's Council in Tel Aviv in 1948.

kept faith with it throughout their Dispersion and never ceased to pray and hope for their return to it and for the restoration in it of their political freedom."

Every generation of Jews, in this view of history, had longed to reestablish itself in the ancient homeland. Over the past two generations, the Zionist movement had begun to realize the dream, sending settlers to Palestine who "made deserts bloom." These settlers built a thriving community, one that controlled its own economy and culture, "loved peace but knew how to defend itself," and brought "the blessings of progress to all the country's inhabitants." In calling for the establishment of a Jewish state, the declaration concluded, the UN had at last recognized "the natural right of the Jewish people to be masters of their own fate, like all other nations, in their own sovereign State." But what of the Arab inhabitants of Palestine? How could they, too, be masters of their own fate? A tragic irony of the contemporary era is that the partial dismantling of one diaspora has led directly to the formation of another.

Israel-Palestine

For Palestine's Arab population, the UN Partition Plan came as a betrayal and a disaster. By the end of the Mandate period in 1948, the Jewish population of Palestine was 650,000, most of them recent immigrants. But the Arab population, at 1.3 million, was twice that number. The Israeli Declaration of Independence pledged that the new state would "foster the development of the country for the benefit of all its inhabitants" and "ensure complete equality of social and political rights to all its inhabitants irrespective of religion, race or sex." But the Palestinian Arabs experienced Zionism as settler colonialism, a type of dispossession and displacement with deep precedents in European history. Palestinians and their supporters today continue to commemorate Israel's Independence Day as *Yawm al-Nakba*—the day of catastrophe.

To secure its independence, Israel had to fight. Civil war broke out between Arabs and Jews in Palestine in 1947. And no sooner had Israel declared its independence the following year than it was attacked by an Arab coalition including Egypt, Syria, Lebanon, Iraq, Transjordan, and Saudi Arabia. Under the armistice demarcation boundaries drawn in 1949 (known as the "Green Line"), the territory controlled by Israel increased by about one-third over the UN Partition Plan, encompassing three-quarters of Mandate Palestine. The Gaza Strip and the West Bank of the Jordan River, still heavily populated by Arabs, were occupied by Egypt and Jordan respectively. During the civil war of 1947/48 and the Arab-Israeli War of 1948/49, about 750,000 Palestinian Arabs—almost two-thirds of the population—fled or were expelled from their homes. Hundreds of Arab villages were depopulated. In the Jewish state that emerged from the war, less than 15 percent of the population was Arab.

About three-quarters of the Arab refugees remained on Palestinian soil, settling alongside the original inhabitants of the heavily

7. **Palestinian women and children flee the town of Jaffa, which later became part of Tel Aviv, in 1948.**

crowded Gaza Strip and the West Bank. The Gaza Strip had some 300,000 residents in 1952, of whom 65 percent were classified as refugees. Egypt administered this territory but did not confer citizenship on its residents. In the West Bank, meanwhile, 40 percent of the 750,000 residents were refugees. In 1949, Jordan extended citizenship to the residents of the West Bank as well as the 100,000 Palestinian refugees within Jordan who had crossed the river into the East Bank. The remaining Palestinian refugees settled in Syria or Lebanon, and in smaller numbers in Egypt and Iraq. These countries did not grant citizenship, insisting that the refugees be allowed to return to Palestine rather than trying to absorb them into their own societies.

The UN defines Palestinian refugee status in a special way. Under the standard definition adopted by the High Commissioner for Refugees (UNHCR), the criterion for refugee status is fear of persecution on grounds of race, religion, politics, nationality, or membership of a particular social group. But the Relief and Works Agency for Palestine Refugees in the Near East (UNRWA) uses geographical and economic criteria instead. Formed in 1950, UNRWA granted refugee status to people who had lived in Palestine for at least two years before the establishment of the state of Israel in 1948, lost their homes and means of livelihood in the ensuing conflict, and fled to one of the places where the UNRWA provided relief (the West Bank, Gaza, Jordan, Syria, and Lebanon). Whereas UNHCR refugees who receive citizenship under the protection of other states lose their refugee status, Palestinians who become citizens elsewhere (mainly in Jordan) do not, as they have not regained their homes and property. They and their descendants remain refugees today.

Matters grew worse for the Palestinians as a result of the Six-Day War of 1967. Defeating the combined forces of Egypt, Jordan, Syria, and Iraq, Israel secured control of the West Bank and Gaza, along with the Sinai Peninsula, east Jerusalem, Shebaa Farms, and the Golan Heights. About 225,000 Palestinians fled the West Bank, crossing the river into Jordan. The UNWRA-registered refugees who stayed in the West Bank under Israeli occupation retained their status as refugees and their Jordanian citizenship (until 1988), but now they were deprived of the protection of the Jordanian state. The indigenous Arabs in the West Bank—those whose families had not been displaced in 1948—lacked both Jordanian protection and refugee status. Some 750,000 UNRWA-registered Palestinian refugees lived in the occupied West Bank in 2012, about the same number of non-refugee Arabs, and 350,000 Israeli settlers.

Conditions in the Gaza Strip are even more precarious than in the West Bank. The ratio of refugees to non-refugees has always been higher in the Gaza Strip, and none of the residents has any form of citizenship. At the same time, migration out of the Gaza Strip has been lower than from the West Bank, allowing for more rapid population increase by natural means. The population of the Gaza Strip stood at about 1.7 million in 2012, of whom 1 million were UNRWA-registered Palestinian refugees. Most of these refugees were born in the Gaza Strip to families displaced earlier.

The refugees in the West Bank and the Gaza Strip make up about one-third of the 5 million Palestinian refugees today. The other refugees live mainly in Jordan, Syria, and Lebanon. One out of every three refugees lives in a camp, of which more than fifty are in operation. The UNRWA does not administer these camps directly, but it provides the residents with humanitarian relief, especially in the form of health and education. Nearly all Palestinians lack citizenship and the protection of a government. Ironically, the main exception is the 1.5 million Arab citizens of the state of Israel (those who do not live in the occupied territories). Today, 11 million people worldwide identify themselves as Palestinian. The largest community outside the Arab world, some 300,000-strong, is in Chile.

How useful or appropriate is the term "diaspora" in the Palestinian case? The Jewish connotations of diaspora are such that Palestinian people are not likely to use the word to describe themselves. Their favored term, *al-Shatat*—signifying displacement and expulsion—is nonetheless strikingly similar in meaning to diaspora. Palestinians use that term to describe a process of expulsion on a colossal scale, the systematic depopulation of towns and villages, and the erasure of their history and culture. Many of the refugees have lived for generations in agonizing proximity to a homeland from which they are permanently excluded, even as Jews from all over the world enjoy a "right of return." While these features are highly distinctive, the Palestinian case has several characteristics that fit within the familiar framework of diaspora. Catastrophic in origin, *al-Shatat* involved dispersal to multiple destinations at once and was accompanied by a strong sense of banishment and exile. Although

Palestinians lacked a coherent nationalist ideology or movement prior to the twentieth century, a powerful form of nationalism emerged in response to the Zionist settlements in the early twentieth century. The Palestinian Liberation Organization (PLO), created in 1964, united a globally dispersed population—from Algiers to London, Beirut to New York, and Damascus to Paris—in a diasporic nationalist movement intent on reacquiring a national territory through violence if necessary. And the desire to return to Palestine was surely intensified by its impossibility.

In the United States and Israel, a vocal minority of academics and activists have tried to envision a post-Zionist Jewish culture. Their concern is that a state defined as a national homeland for the Jewish people, with a Law of Return based primarily on bloodlines, cannot be truly democratic. One group of scholars, known as the "new historians" set out to debunk the prevailing narrative of Israeli history, especially concerning the nature of Palestinian Arabs' displacement. Other academic critics see the very attempt to root national identity in a territorially bounded state as an abandonment of Jewishness. Zionism, they argue, represented a sharp break with two thousand years of history by seeking to contain Jewishness within a nation-state.

Insisting that the unique virtues and accomplishments of the Jewish people lie precisely in diaspora, these critics emphasize cultural difference and open-ended coexistence over a national identity based on the possession of territory. From this perspective, non-Israeli Jews today might better be described as a global people rather than a diasporic people. Within Israel, meanwhile, some ultra-Orthodox Jewish groups, such as the Naturei Karta and the Reb Arelach, deny the legitimacy of the state on the grounds than man alone cannot bring about the "ingathering" of the Jews and that the true Israel will be restored only through divine providence.

At an abstract theoretical level, these are fascinating arguments. Yet the very open-endedness that cultural critics celebrate, the insistence on retaining the particularity of Jewish culture without a nation-state, can be acutely double-edged in practice. It accounts for not only the unique historical accomplishments of Jewish civilization but also its terrible vulnerability. The very lack of rootedness and belonging provoked the anti-Semites; they hated Jews for retaining a unique identity within the boundaries of existing nation-states. For the Zionists, too, the absence of national affiliation was the problem: what they wanted was a Jewish state with its own territory. And how could the Jewish people survive without such a state after the Holocaust? From a Palestinian perspective, however, the price of Jewish statehood has been incalculable.

The Law of Return

Diaspora

Israel's relations with the Palestinians stand in sharp contrast with its policy toward Jews around the world who wish to enter the country. In its Declaration of Independence, Israel acknowledged its reliance on continued migration and financial support from Jewish communities globally. The declaration proclaimed that Israel "would open the gates of the homeland wide to every Jew" to facilitate "the Ingathering of the Exiles." The Law of Return (1950) confirmed the right of all Jews to settle in Israel. An amendment to the law passed in 1970 stated that anyone who was Jewish by birth or conversion, who had a Jewish parent, grandparent, or spouse, or who was married to a child or grandchild of a Jew, was guaranteed the right to migrate to Israel and to become an Israeli citizen on arrival. Using the word "return"—as distinct from immigration— reinforced the Jewish claim to Palestine as an ancestral homeland. Between 1948 and 1999 some 3 million *olim* came to Israel. Among them were the entire community of 49,000 Yemenite Jews, who were flown to Israel in 1949 and 1950 in Operation on Wings of Eagles. The name alluded to the prophesy in Isaiah 40:31 that God would return the children of Israel to Zion on the wings of eagles. Similar operations to transport communities of Jews from Arab countries to Israel followed in the 1950s and 1960s.

One of the most dramatic cases of repatriation was that of the Ethiopian Jews in 1991. Ethiopia has a unique Christian heritage but also a distinct Jewish tradition. Members of both religions in Ethiopia find inspiration in the *Kebra Negast* ("Glory of Kings"), a holy book that draws from the Bible, the Koran, apocryphal sources, and local folklore. According to the *Kebra Negast*, the Ethiopians are God's chosen people. King Solomon and the Queen of Sheba had a son, Menelik, who was later crowned king of Ethiopia and returned to his kingdom with the Ark of the Covenant. The Ethiopian Jews claim descent from this line. They believe that when Menelik and his followers returned to Ethiopia, they came to a river and separated into two groups. Those who crossed the river became Christians and those who did not remained Jews. The Christian majority eventually deprived the Ethiopian Jews of the right to own land and referred to them as *falasha*, a pejorative term meaning landless (and, by extension, strangers, outsiders, or exiles). They referred to themselves as the *Beta Israel*—the Community of Israel.

Scholars and religious teachers disagree on the origins and authenticity of the Ethiopian Jews. In 1973 Israel's Sephardic chief rabbi recognized them as a remnant of the lost tribe of Dan, which entitled them to the privileges of the Law of Return. His Ashkenazi counterpart issued a similar judgment two years later. Whatever their origins, the *Beta Israel* had practiced a form of Judaism in isolation in the mountains of northern Ethiopia for many centuries. They continued to follow strict dietary proscriptions, sacrifice sheep at Passover, and circumcise on the eighth day, but they spoke Amharic rather than Hebrew and they prayed in Ge'ez, the classical language of Ethiopia, while facing Jerusalem.

In the 1970s, following the overthrow of Emperor Haile Selassie's government by Marxist insurgents, Jews in both Israel and the United States agitated for the "return" of the Ethiopian Jews to Israel. With Ethiopia ravaged by war and famine in the 1980s and 1990s, Israel organized a series of airlifts from the Sudanese camps in which the Ethiopian Jews sought refuge. Operation Moses brought more than 7,000 Ethiopian Jews to Israel in 1984. Finally, in Operation Solomon, in May 1991, the Israeli Air Force transported 14,324 Jews from Addis Ababa, the capital of Ethiopia, in a complex two-day operation involving thirty-four aircraft. On arrival, they were greeted by Israel's prime minister Yitzhak Shamir and high-level members of his government. Nearly all of Ethiopia's Jews relocated. More than 130,000 live in Israel today, about one-third of whom were born there.

Ethiopian Jews of *Beta Israel* origin whose ancestors converted to Christianity were not so fortunate. Thousands of these converts, known as *Falash Mura*, abandoned their homes and possessions in hopes of joining friends and relatives in Operation Solomon. But, having reverted to Judaism only quite recently, they have no automatic right of return. Most of the *Falash Mura* have been languishing in refugee camps in Ethiopia since 1991, waiting for permission to enter Israel. Some have secured permission on grounds of family reunification under the Law of Entry, which regulates immigration by those who are not covered by the Law of Return.

By far the biggest single group of *olim* to arrive in Israel were those who left the former Soviet Union in the 1990s. At the time of its dissolution, the Soviet Union included about 2 million Jews. In the Soviet system of ethnic classification, citizens had their nationality inscribed in their passports, with "Jewish" as one of the categories. Being classified as Jewish led to discrimination in education and employment, but it also held the possibility of emigration to Israel. Most Soviet Jews were not Jewish by strict rabbinical standards: their ethnic status was based on their father's nationality, contradicting the central Mosaic principle of matrilineal descent. Spouses of Jewish men were accorded Jewish status based on their husband's surname alone. In a society in which overt religious practice had long been discouraged, the majority of Russian Jews were secular. They did not attend synagogues, study

8. In Operation Solomon, the Israeli Air Force transports Ethiopian Jews to Israel in May 1991.

the Hebrew Bible, observe the high holidays, or adhere to Jewish dietary practices.

Unversed in Judaism as a religion, Soviet Jews nonetheless cherished their Jewishness as an identity. Under the Law of Return, they were entitled to go to Israel and, once the Soviet Union collapsed, they were able to do so in large numbers. About 1 million Russian Jews went to Israel in the 1990s, many hoping it would be a stepping-stone to the United States. The influx increased the population of Israel by 20 percent, revitalized the economy, and reshaped national politics. Unlike previous *olim*, however, the Russian Jews showed little interest in learning Hebrew or assimilating in other ways. Retaining their language and culture, they read their own Russian newspapers, watched Russian television by satellite, and built distinct ethnic enclaves. Their presence raised pressing questions about what it means to be Israeli and what it means to be Jewish.

A commonly accepted estimate for the number of Jews in the world today is 13.5 million. More than 80 percent live in Israel or the United States—about 5.5 million in each case—and most of the remainder in Europe (1.5 million), with smaller populations in Canada, Mexico, Argentina, Africa, and elsewhere. Put another way, almost 60 percent of Jews live outside Israel in today's "Jewish Diaspora." According to some scholars, in both America and France, the decision to remain "in diaspora," combined with the relative decline of anti-Semitism since World War II, has significantly undermined Jewish identity outside Israel. From this perspective, Jewishness is being diluted into a form of symbolic ethnicity, conforming to the pattern of assimilation followed by other ethnic groups. Yet many American Jews would not describe themselves that way. Israel is not the center of their lives, but they see themselves as no less Jewish for that. Far from pining way in exile, they are at home, like Jeremiah's Jews in Babylon, where they are. At the same time, many of them remain engaged with Israel, some as critics and others as supporters. Since 1951 Israel has raised $25 billion in "diaspora bonds"—a mixture of relatively low-yield investment and patriotic donation—from Jews living outside the state.

For most migrant groups, unlike modern Jews, "going home" has either presented formidable obstacles, or it has simply been impossible in practice. Yet, even when return was metaphorical rather literal, the idea could be deeply inspirational. A significant number of people of African origin, for example, crossed the Atlantic and settled in West Africa. The vast majority could never hope to do so, even if they wanted to. But the idea of a "return to Africa" was nonetheless a potent spiritual and political force in their struggle against racism and injustice in the Atlantic world.

African homelands

The idea of African unity, and a homeland for people of African origin in exile, emerged among slaves and their descendants in the Atlantic world. It developed in songs, sermons, and folklore, and in the autobiographies and political tracts of the black elite. Advocates of a return to Africa believed that the returnees would bring with them the virtues of commerce and Christianity and, in so doing, redeem all African people. In the nineteenth century, however, this vision was always sharply double-edged. It appealed in different ways both to people of African origin who wished to move to Africa of their own accord and to whites who sponsored colonization schemes in order to rid their countries of an undesirable free black population.

The British founded the colony of Sierra Leone as a refuge for African Americans who had taken their side during the American Revolutionary War. Britain had offered freedom to American slaves in return for their support; once the war was lost, not all of these slaves could simply be abandoned. About 3,000 black loyalists sailed from New York City to Nova Scotia in 1783, but they struggled to survive in an environment unsuited to agriculture and featuring many former slave owners. Meanwhile in London, a group of abolitionists was planning to relocate some of the city's black poor to a suitable location in West Africa. The first attempt to plant a colony in 1787 was a disaster. But it inspired a second attempt in 1792, featuring about 1,000 of the Nova Scotians, which resulted in the establishment of a permanent colony in Freetown. Sierra Leone soon became a magnet for returnees from the United States and the Caribbean.

Among those who saw the potential of Sierra Leone as a homeland for African Americans was the Massachusetts sea captain Paul Cuffe. Cuffe reached Freetown on his first expedition to West Africa in 1811. He envisaged a great new African nation, populated by industrious black migrants from the Americas with commercial ties extending across the Atlantic world. Cuffe returned to Freetown on a second expedition in 1815 with thirty-eight colonists, whose passage and expenses he helped finance. At the time of his death two years later, he was still making plans for a mass migration to Africa. Although this dream proved unrealistic, Cuffe prefigured Marcus Garvey to a remarkable degree. A century before Garvey established his Black Star Line, Cuffe had a fleet of ships ready to take African Americans back to Africa to redeem their homeland.

By the time of Cuffe's death, African American advocates of return faced an uncomfortable dilemma. Other Americans were even more eager to see blacks leave, but for quite different reasons. The American Colonization Society (ACS), founded in 1816 with the support of leading political figures such as James Monroe and Henry Clay, saw no future for freed slaves in America. Cuffe was open to working with the ACS, as were Richard Allen of the African Methodist Episcopal Church and other black leaders. But African American opinion, at least in the North, soon turned sharply against the ACS, discrediting the idea of return for more than a generation. Most free blacks in the North strongly rejected the idea of colonization from this point on, realizing that it had become a pretext for removing them from the country. There is some evidence, though, that the idea remained somewhat more popular in the South, where any escape from slavery would have been welcome.

The ACS, meanwhile, pressed ahead with its plans to rid the United States of unwanted free blacks. In 1820 the Society colonized a region to the east of Sierra Leone, which became known as Liberia. More than 13,000 African Americans had moved there by 1867 with the assistance of the ACS. The colonists who provided the economic and political leadership—among them Edward Blyden of St. Thomas and John Russwurm, the Jamaican-born former editor of New York's black abolitionist newspaper, *Freedom's Journal*, who broke with the dominant line of that publication and came out in favor of colonization—differentiated themselves sharply from the indigenous African population. These men saw themselves as building an ideal black American society in Africa, an outpost of Christian civilization in a pagan land. In 1847 the colonists founded the Republic of Liberia, establishing a government modeled on that of the United States and naming their capital city Monrovia, after President James Monroe. While most African Americans who migrated to Liberia did so before the Civil War, a few thousand moved there in the 1880s and 1890s in a grassroots movement triggered by racial violence, disfranchisement, and segregation, and infused by ideas of black nationalism.

Some former slaves also migrated to West Africa from Brazil between 1830 and 1888. Lacking a formal emigration program comparable to that of the ACS, the Brazilians generally had to fund their own passage and resettlement. Nonetheless, about 8,000 of them made their way across the Atlantic Ocean. They settled in port cities such as Lagos, Uidah, Porto Novo, and Agoué. Their descendants in Benin and Nigeria are known today as Agudas, the Yoruba word for Catholics. In Ghana, they are known as Tabom, deriving from the Portuguese phrase "'tá bom" (a contraction of "está bom," it's good), the customary response to the question "how are you?" or "how is it going?" In parts of West Africa, Brazilian influence is still evident in styles of food and architecture.

The call for a return to Africa took a radical form in the United States in the 1850s. Martin Delany, a journalist, physician, and abolitionist who is widely regarded in America as the "father of black nationalism," came to believe that black people could control their own economic destiny and achieve political sovereignty only where they constituted a majority of the population. In 1835, after attending the National Convention of Men of Color in Philadelphia, Delany conceived the idea of setting up a "Black Israel" on the east coast of Africa. In his book *The Condition, Elevation, Emigration, and Destiny of the Colored People of the United States, Politically Considered* (1852) and a manifesto titled "Political Destiny of the Colored Race on the American Continent" (1854), Delany argued that blacks had no future in the United States. They should found a new nation elsewhere, he said, perhaps in the West Indies or South America. He eventually set his sights on West Africa and sailed for Liberia in 1859 in search of a territory in which to establish a colony.

Little came of this endeavor, and by 1860 Delany was back in the United States. During the Civil War, he recruited and commanded African American troops, becoming the first black field officer in the U.S. Army in 1865, with a commission as major. After the war, Delany worked for the Freedmen's Bureau and agitated for the redistribution of planters' land to the former slaves. With the abandonment of Reconstruction, he revived his interest in colonization, but again to little practical effect. African Americans continued to resist colonization for the most part, aware that it could too readily serve the purposes of their oppressors. But Delany left an ideological legacy emphasizing racial purity, black separatism, and an Afrocentric cultural identity. Like Paul Cuffe, he was an important forerunner of Marcus Garvey.

Marcus Mosiah Garvey—whose middle name was a variant of Moses—led the most important "Back to Africa" movement of the early twentieth century. Garvey called not simply for repatriation as a long-term goal but also for pride in black skin and African heritage. He never visited Africa, and his idea of return had strong spiritual and figurative dimensions. In a speech in Madison Square Garden in 1924, Garvey announced his hope that people would one day rest their weary backs by the banks of the Niger "and sing our songs and chant our hymns to the God of Ethiopia." Most of his audience knew they would never see Africa for themselves. But this realization surely intensified, rather than diminished, the feeling inspired by the biblical allusion.

Chanting down Babylon

Marcus Garvey is the principal prophet of the Rastafari movement. Before leaving Jamaica for the last time in 1935 to settle in London, Garvey is said to have told his followers, "Look to Africa for the crowning of a black king, he shall be the redeemer." The Rastafari took these words as prophesy and came to believe that Haile Selassie, the emperor of Ethiopia from 1930 to 1974, was the second coming of the Messiah. Born Tafari Makonnen, the emperor bore the title "Ras" (duke or prince) before ascending to the throne. He traced his lineage via the *Kebra Negast* back to Solomon and Sheba, and their son Menelik, who brought the Ark of the Covenant from Jerusalem and made the Ethiopians God's new chosen people. As Solomon, in this reading of religious history, was an ancestor of Christ, the kings of Ethiopia were therefore divine. In 1930 Ras Tafari assumed the titles "His Imperial Majesty Haile Selassie I, Conquering Lion of the Tribe of Judah, King of Kings, Emperor, Elect of God," words that recur like mantras in the Rastafari culture and in the more religious forms of reggae music. Neither Haile Selassie nor Marcus Garvey, it should be noted, participated in the Rastafari movement. The emperor initially knew nothing of the faith dedicated to him, while Garvey was quite critical.

For the Rastafari, Ethiopia was the Promised Land. In the religious and literary traditions that emerged from Atlantic slavery, Ethiopia and Zion were used as terms interchangeable with Africa.

Jamaicans, too, used Ethiopia to refer to Africa in general, but for them the actual nation of Ethiopia came to occupy a special place. As one of the few countries in Africa independent of European rule—at least until the Italians invaded in the 1930s—Ethiopia was a source of inspiration. The Ethiopian Orthodox Church, of which Haile Selassie was a lifelong member, traced its roots to the fourth century CE.

The Rastafari found ample biblical evidence for the divinity of Haile Selassie. They interpreted the reference in Psalm 68:31 to Ethiopia stretching out its hands to God as signifying Ethiopia's acceptance of the Ark of the Covenant and the redemptive role in history that came with it. And they cited the passage in Revelation 5:2–5 where the Lion of Judah opens the seven seals, thereby unleashing the historical forces that will bring about the end times.

In the 1930s, a man by the name of Leonard Howell began selling postcards of Haile Selassie in the slums of Kingston, Jamaica, which he claimed could be used as "passports" to Ethiopia. Howell declared the emperor's divinity as early as 1933. Haile Selassie, he declared, had returned to earth to kill Nebuchadnezzar's image (a symbol of Babylon named for the king who had destroyed the First Temple in 586 CE). People of African descent in exile in the West, Howell claimed, were one of the lost tribes of Israel. In a book called *The Promised Key* (1935), he elaborated on these claims and predicted that blacks would be repatriated to Africa. Imprisoned for seditious activities, Howell led his followers into the wilderness after his release. They founded a commune called Pinnacle in the hills outside Kingston, and it was there, in the 1940s and 1950s, that the Rastafari movement assumed its familiar form.

At Pinnacle, the commune members let their hair grow wild until it gradually became tangled or "locked." These "dreadlocks," which came to typify the Rastafari movement, were the product not of careful styling and braiding but the opposite. Left to its own devices, hair naturally tangles and locks. The Rastafari came to be known as "locksmen" or "natty dreads," with the word "dread" signifying both fear of the Lord and alienation from Babylon. Seeing themselves as Israelites sent into slavery and exile, the Rastafari based their dietary and hygienic practices on Mosaic law. A potent strain of marijuana known as ganja or sensimilla (from the Spanish *sin semillas*, without seeds) assumed sacred status among them. The herb provided temporary release from alienation and insights into the cosmic and eternal. When they returned from the wilderness, the Rastafari roamed the streets denouncing Jamaican society or, as they put it, "chanting down Babylon."

The ultimate release from Babylon would be to return physically to Africa. The Rastafari believed, at least at first, that black people would eventually be repatriated en masse from the countries where they had been enslaved. An early step toward realizing this goal came in 1938 when the Ethiopian World Federation (EWF), established in New York the previous year, opened a branch in Jamaica. Organized with the intention of assisting Ethiopia in its struggle against Italian colonialism, the EWF proclaimed the unity and solidarity of all people of African origin. In 1955, the EWF announced that Emperor Selassie had granted five hundred acres of land for settlement by black people in the West who had assisted Ethiopia in the war. If this plan succeeded, other grants would follow. This news, which came at a time when thousands of Jamaicans were leaving home for the cold unknown of England—relocating from one part of Babylon to another—caused great excitement among the Rastafari. "Repatriation Now!" became the cry.

When it was announced that Haile Selassie would visit Jamaica for four days in April 1966, expectations peaked that mass repatriation would follow. The Rastafari did not organize the visit, which was a by-product of an invitation by Eric Williams, the historian of slavery and prime minister of Trinidad and Tobago. But they turned out in huge numbers to welcome the emperor. Isaiah 43:6 held the key: "I will say to the north, Give up; and to the south,

Keep not back: bring my sons from far, and my daughters from the ends of the earth." But the emperor's visit did not trigger a mass repatriation. Younger members of the movement soon embraced the idea of "liberation before migration," concentrating on winning freedom and justice in Jamaica as a prelude to return.

The idea of return did not have to be literal; it could be even more powerful in allegorical form. It was in popular culture, and especially music, that the connection with Africa assumed its most influential dimensions. The Rastafari movement gave rise to a new type of music called *nyabinghi*, which owed much of its origin to the *kumina* style of singing and dancing practiced by the slaves. Among the most important practitioners of *nyabinghi* was Count Ossie (Oswald Williams), whose rhythmic drumming and vocal chanting, derived from nineteenth-century slave music, was designed to induce states of heightened spirituality. Count Ossie set up a Rastafari community in east Kingston in the 1950s. His group, Mystic Revelation of Rastafari, was hugely influential, especially their 1973 album *Grounation*.

Although reggae music incorporated *nyabinghi* elements, it evolved more directly from the ska and rock steady styles of the 1960s. Many reggae stars today, despite their braided dreadlocks and obligatory references to Marcus Garvey and Haile Selassie, have little or no connection to the Rastafari movement. Stricter adherents of the movement seek to dissociate themselves from popular music. But the connection between reggae and Rastafari is inescapable, because the greatest reggae star of all, Bob Marley, was a convert to the movement.

Marley was born in 1945, in the same Jamaican parish as Marcus Garvey. In the early 1960s he formed a band with Peter Tosh and Bunny Livingston (later Bunny Wailer). They called themselves Bob Marley and the Wailers. By 1975 Marley and his group had converted to the Rastafari faith. Haile Selassie died that year, but in a series of "roots reggae" albums, beginning with *Natty Dread* and continuing through *Rastaman Vibration*, *Exodus*, *Survival*, and *Uprising*, Marley made the Rastafari message popular all over the world. He died in 1981, at the age of thirty-six. The funeral was the largest in Jamaican history. Lying in a bronze coffin, Marley held a Bible in his right hand—opened to Psalm 23, "The Lord Is My Shepherd"—and a guitar in his left, wearing the tam of the Twelve Tribes of Israel, a Rastafari sect.

Reggae soon evolved into a number of styles and went global. Burning Spear continued to develop the Afrocentric roots reggae style. Lee "Scratch" Perry ("The Upsetter") developed dub reggae and became one of the most influential producers in both Jamaica and England. Jah Love Muzik International, led by Brigadier Jerry and Ilawi, propagated the message of the Twelve Tribes of Israel in a new, improvised deejay style. Bootleg cassettes of their powerful live performances, steeped in biblical lore, circulated throughout London and New York as well as Jamaica. Artists such as Yellowman, Eek-a-Mouse, and Barrington Levi pioneered the dancehall style, which eventually gave way to raggamuffin (ragga) and exercised a decisive influence on hip-hop and rap. The religious content of reggae music gradually became muted or formulaic, but it was music more than any other cultural force that popularized the idea of African diasporic unity in the late twentieth century.

Afro-Caribbean musicians in England were major innovators in this respect. Jamaicans had been migrating to England since the 1940s, only to experience racism and intense alienation there. A vibrant Rastafari movement emerged in London, Birmingham, and other English cities in parallel with developments in Jamaica. Caribbean reggae stars began and ended their European tours in England. Homegrown bands such as Steel Pulse developed a hard-edged style of protest music, while artists such as Lynton Kwesi Johnson, Sister Netifa, and Benjamin Zephaniah adopted an equally radical stance in the new genre of dub poetry. Ska and reggae rhythms had a huge influence on English two-tone and punk music. The bhangra music imported to Britain by Punjabi immigrants, meanwhile, merged with reggae dancehall rhythms in the work of artists like Apache Indian and Bally Sagoo.

Completing the circle, reggae also took hold in Africa. In albums such as *Survival*, Bob Marley had embraced a militant Pan-African nationalism. The anti-racist song "War," from *Rastaman Vibration*, which set to music a speech by Haile Selassie before the UN General Assembly in 1963, inspired revolutionaries throughout Africa, and especially in Zimbabwe (then Rhodesia). Marley's performance in Harare on Zimbabwe's Independence Day, April 18, 1980, had a significant impact on African music. Alpha Blondy of the Ivory Coast, who melded West African melodies with the Jamaican roots style, became the first big name in African reggae. More recently, Askia Modibo of Mali has combined local pentatonic musical structures with reggae beats, female backing vocals, a prominent horn section, and potent protest lyrics, achieving fame in France as well as throughout Africa. Reggae became the diasporic sound par excellence. In music, at least, the dream of a return to Africa was fulfilled.

Chapter 5
A global concept

In the contemporary era of globalization, diaspora has become an extraordinarily popular word. The reasons for its popularity lie in a series of developments since World War II. In the era of decolonization, globally scattered communities—most notably those of African origin—forged new bonds of solidarity. Many migrant groups or their descendants—especially Asians—were uprooted and forced to relocate as the countries where they lived moved toward independence. In addition to these "repeat migrants," the contemporary era featured a new class of internationally recognized refugees. The number of people on the move globally has increased significantly in recent decades, leading some commentators to proclaim a new era of international migration or an age of diaspora. These claims, however, can be assessed only in historical perspective. A final distinguishing feature of the contemporary era is the efforts by various states to reach out to their overseas populations, tapping into their considerable financial and political resources in return for investment incentives and new forms of dual or flexible citizenship. As a concept for helping people understand these recent developments—decolonization, repeat migration, refugee status, increased numbers, and government outreach efforts—diaspora has considerable explanatory power. In many ways, it is an ideal concept for a global age.

Repeat migrants and refugees

The age of decolonization, which began in the mid-twentieth century, gave rise to new kinds of migration. Among these was a pattern that can be called "repeat migration." Because of the resentment of indigenous populations, many Asian migrants were forced to move from the places where they or their ancestors had settled. As colonies in Asia and East Africa aspired to or achieved independence, members of their Chinese and Indian communities encountered considerable economic and political hostility from local populations. At its most severe, this hostility triggered expulsions or involuntary migrations of the kind the concept of diaspora is well suited to explain.

Throughout Southeast Asia, the ethnic Chinese prospered economically in the twentieth century but remained vulnerable to nativist backlash. In Malaysia, Indonesia, Thailand, Vietnam, and elsewhere, the Chinese controlled a disproportionate share of business. As early as 1914, King Rama VI of Siam denounced the Chinese as the "Jews of the East." Hostility toward the Chinese intensified during the Great Depression. Siam adopted the name Thailand in 1938 to emphasize a national identity separate from that of its sizable Chinese minority. Chinese businesses faced tight regulation during the coming decades, though the ethnic Chinese in Thailand today are unusually well integrated.

Anti-Chinese prejudice was most severe in Indonesia. The ethnic Chinese made up only about 4 percent of the population at the end of World War II, but they still amounted to fully 3 million people. The Indonesian rebellion against Dutch colonial rule in 1945–1949 unleashed a wave of anti-Chinese violence. As Indonesia consolidated its independence in the 1950s and 1960s, more than 100,000 ethnic Chinese fled the country, many on vessels provided by the Chinese government. But they soon discovered that they were not welcome in China either. Like so many returnees before and since, they found themselves trapped between two cultures and at home in neither.

Anti-Chinese agitation in Indonesia intensified during the turmoil of the 1960s. Thousands of ethnic Chinese were killed or driven from their homes during the anti-Communist bloodletting of 1965–1966. When General Suharto consolidated power, the policy of forced or encouraged migration gave way to one of simultaneously diluting Chinese ethnic identity while tolerating the Chinese business elite for the advantages it brought to the economy. The Suharto government banned the Chinese script, discouraged the speaking of Chinese in public, closed Chinese-language schools, and outlawed the celebration of Chinese festivals. Many Chinese changed their names, but their identity cards recorded their ethnic origins. At the same time, the Chinese elite retained close links with the government, and several well-connected businessmen became very rich and powerful. The extent of anti-Chinese sentiment was starkly evident in the riots that toppled Suharto in 1998. The rioters looted and burned Chinese businesses, attacked and killed Chinese men, and systematically raped Chinese women. Once again, tens of thousands of people fled the country.

Indians faced an even more concerted backlash during the era of decolonization. Anti-Indian sentiment in Burma intensified with the onset of the Great Depression and the emergence of an anti-colonial movement in the 1930s. When the Chettiar caste of merchant bankers began to foreclose on mortgages to local cultivators, taking over significant amounts of land, Burmese activists turned against all Indians. In 1930, following a strike by Indian dockworkers, mobs killed at least 120 Indians in Rangoon and injured as many as 2,000. More attacks followed throughout the decade. During World War II, half a million Indians left Burma, trekking overland to Assam. When Burma became independent in 1948, Indians were denied citizenship. Most of the remaining Indian population was expelled in 1962.

Indians faced similar problems when Ceylon (known since 1972 as Sri Lanka) became independent in 1948. The South Indian Tamil population was excluded from the protections of the new constitution by the Sinhalese majority. Denied citizenship in India as well, these Tamils remained stateless until 1964, when India and Ceylon agreed on terms for their repatriation. Over the next two decades, hundreds of thousands of Tamils moved "back" to India, a land their ancestors had left generations earlier, in which they now found themselves as strangers. Anti-Tamil pogroms, meanwhile, continued in Sri Lanka. Tamil militants fought a hugely destructive but ultimately unsuccessful war of independence between 1983 and 2009, resulting in massive internal displacement and further repatriation to India.

In East Africa, South Asians faced particular suspicion from native populations in the wake of independence. Denied the right to own land by British policy, they concentrated in urban locations where they worked in business and in the imperial service. They tended to be more skilled and better educated than Indian migrants elsewhere and occupied an intermediate niche between the British elite and the indigenous people. Although Asians accounted for only a tiny minority of the local populations—about 2 percent in Kenya and 1 percent in Uganda and Tanzania—Africans came to see them as colonial collaborators. With the onset of independence, Indians began moving capital overseas and some took British rather than local citizenship. Both moves stoked the fires of postcolonial resentment. The newly independent governments of Kenya, Uganda, and Tanzania responded by excluding Asians from jobs and services.

The result was an exodus from East Africa. At first, this movement was largely voluntary. About 23,000 Kenyan Asians moved to Britain in 1965–1967. Alarmed by the growing scale of this migration, the government excluded British Commonwealth passport holders from entering the country unless they could demonstrate existing "patrial links" in Britain (a parent or grandparent who was born, adopted, or naturalized in the United

Kingdom). Meanwhile, in Uganda, an even more concerted anti-Asian campaign was getting under way. About 24,000 Asians left Uganda between 1969 and 1971. Most of them managed to make their way to the United Kingdom, with smaller numbers settling in the United States, Canada, India, and Pakistan.

The Ugandan crisis reached its peak in August 1972 when President Idi Amin revealed that God had told him, in a dream, that all Asians must be expelled from the country within ninety days. Arrangements were made to accommodate these refugees in various Commonwealth countries—29,000 in the United Kingdom, 10,000 in India, and 8,000 in Canada. Another 6,000 settled in continental Europe and 3,000 in the United States. Most had to leave their money and belongings behind. The so-called "Ugandan Asians" tended to be better educated and had higher levels of skill than the Pakistanis and Bangladeshis who arrived in Britain in the 1950s and 1960s. But they faced intense hostility from Britons who insisted that their towns and cities were already saturated with Asian immigrants.

Fiji's independence from Britain in 1970, meanwhile, intensified a long-standing ethnic conflict there. People of Indian descent slightly outnumbered native Fijians, and there had long been considerable tension between them. Resentment against perceived Indo-Fijian privilege led to a military coup against the Indian-led government in 1987, and an attempted coup in 2000, accompanied by widespread violence against Indians. Large numbers of Indo-Fijians left for Australia, New Zealand, the United States, and Canada. As a result, people of Indian origin now constitute a minority of the population in Fiji. Asians also fled the former Dutch colony of Suriname (Dutch Guiana) after it achieved independence in 1975. About 40 percent of the population (300,000 people) was of Indian descent and half of them relocated to the Netherlands. They were not forced to leave, but they were fearful of ethnic tensions, skeptical about their postcolonial prospects, and eager to avail of Holland's liberal citizenship laws.

Some of the migrants forced out by postcolonial resentment—most notably the ethnic Chinese—won recognition and protection by the UN as refugees. In a generic sense, there have been refugees as long as there have been wars, plagues, and famines. But the period since World War II saw the emergence of formal definitions and policies and a greatly heightened global awareness of the issue. The office of the United Nations High Commissioner for Refugees (UNHCR) in Geneva, established in 1950, provides humanitarian relief and seeks to protect the human rights of all refugees (except Palestinian Arabs displaced by the formation of the state of Israel, and their descendants, who come under the separate jurisdiction of the United Nations Relief and Works Agency, UNRWA). The refugee question has drawn global attention to mass migration and to the idea of diaspora.

While the origins of refugee policy lie mainly in World War II, the Vietnam War brought the question to international notice as never before. Among the 3 million people who left Vietnam in the turmoil that engulfed the region between 1975 and the early 1990s were significant numbers of ethnic Chinese (*Hoa*). Concentrated in the Saigon area, the *Hoa* accounted for only 5 percent of Vietnam's population in 1975 but controlled three-quarters of its trade. When the war ended, the new regime banned private trade, closed businesses, confiscated foreign currency, and forced businessmen to join the armed forces, move to the countryside as farmers, or enter "re-education" camps. As the most dynamic element of the economy, the *Hoa* suffered most directly from these measures.

Vietnam's Chinese population soon sought refuge elsewhere. In 1978 about 150,000 migrated overland into China. Beijing objected to Vietnam's treatment of the ethnic Chinese, and relations between the two countries deteriorated. When Vietnam invaded Cambodia in 1978, China responded by invading Vietnam. The ethnic Chinese in northern Vietnam, denounced as a potential "fifth column," were forced to relocate from coastal

9. Fleeing persecution in Vietnam, a group of refugees arrives in Malaysia after their boat capsized offshore in 1978.

cities to the remote interior, or were allowed to leave the country in return for substantial payments. Tens of thousands took to the sea in desperation, seeking refuge in Malaysia, Thailand, and elsewhere. About 250,000 *Hoa* made their way to Hong Kong or mainland China in 1979.

The ethnic Chinese were part of the larger exodus from Vietnam often referred to by the shorthand term "boat people." Huge numbers perished at sea or lost their possessions to pirates. Asian countries were reluctant to take the refugees, but the UNHCR eventually set up camps for those who landed in Hong Kong, Malaysia, Thailand, Indonesia, and the Philippines. The United States accepted more than 800,000 Vietnamese refugees, and Canada and Australia 135,000 each. The ordeal of the boat people, their continued suffering in the camps, and the arrival of large numbers of Vietnamese and Cambodians in the United States focused international attention on the refugee question. In December 2000, the UN declared June 20 World Refugee Day.

In 2010, UNHCR classified 10.5 million people as refugees (in addition to the 4.6 million Palestinian Arabs with UNRWA status). The largest number of UNHCR refugees—3 million—were Afghans. More than 6 million people left Afghanistan in the decade after the Soviets invaded in 1979, mainly for Pakistan and Iran. About 5.7 million refugees returned to Afghanistan in the decade after 2002, but others continued to leave following the American invasion. About 1.7 million Afghan migrants remained in Pakistan in 2010 as recognized refugees, along with perhaps another 1 million who were there informally or illegally. Refugees from Iraq were the second largest refugee group in 2010 (1.7 million), followed by Somalia (770,000), the Democratic Republic of Congo (477,000), and Myanmar (416,000). Contrary to common perception, most refugees do not live in the West. Eighty percent of the world's refugees in 2010 lived in developing countries. Slightly more than half were in Asia, almost a quarter in Africa, and only 15 percent in Europe and 4 percent in North America. Pakistan, with 1.9 million, hosted more refugees than any other country. Iran and Syria had about 1 million refugees each, and both Jordan and Germany had about half a million.

In addition to refugees, UNHCR provides assistance to an even larger category of "persons of concern." This category includes failed asylum seekers deported to their home countries who need protection, along with an ever-increasing number of "internally displaced people" (IDPs) who remain within their own countries and consequently lack the protection of international law. In 2010, UNHCR provided protection and assistance to an estimated 14.7 million IDPs cut off from their homes by war, famine, or environmental problems, along with 2.9 million IDPs who had managed to return to their places of origin. The agency identified an additional 3.5 million stateless persons, scattered across sixty-five countries, though it estimated that the true number was closer to 12 million. Between refugees, IDPs, and other stateless persons, the number of involuntary migrants probably exceeded 40 million.

Contemporary migration

In 2000 the United Nations General Assembly declared December 18 International Migrants Day. Noting "the large and increasing number of migrants in the world," the declaration insisted that migrants were entitled to the same rights as all humans. The standard definition of an international migrant is a person who has moved from one country to another and remained there for at least a year. By that measure, an estimated 3.1 percent of the world's population in 2010 were international migrants. This figure may seem low on first sight, but 3.1 percent of 7 billion is 217 million (a figure that includes refugees, but not IDPs). If all these international migrants moved to an unoccupied country, that country would be the fifth most populous on earth—exceeded only by China, India, the United States, and Indonesia.

Although the UN proclamation was correct in stating that the number of international migrants is large and increasing, this formulation can also be misleading. The number of migrants has certainly grown in recent decades, but the rate of global migration is not necessarily greater than it was in earlier periods. The term "diaspora" owes much of its current popularity to an uncritical belief that the world has recently entered an era of unprecedented population mobility, part of the globalization process that characterizes the contemporary era. But just as the origins of globalization go back several centuries, contemporary migration cannot be understood outside its deeper historical context.

The United States, for example, admitted more than 10 million legal immigrants in the first decade of the twenty-first century. In addition, an unknown number entered the country without papers or stayed after their temporary visas expired. But even if these irregular immigrants are included, boosting the overall figure to the maximum conceivable figure of 1.5 million a year, the rate of immigration (i.e., the annual inflow as a percentage of the population as a whole) would still be significantly lower today than it was a century ago. In the opening decade of the twentieth century, the United States admitted roughly 9 million immigrants, about the same as in 1901–1910. In gross terms, the figures for each decade are roughly comparable. But the population of the United States in 1900 was only 75 million, compared to 315 million in 2013. Although Americans are currently living through the greatest wave of immigration in their history, immigration had a much greater impact on their society in the past.

This sort of historical perspective can also illuminate the character of contemporary global migration as a whole. The world has certainly experienced an upsurge in migration in recent decades, measured by absolute numbers. An estimated 7 million to 8 million people are now migrating across international borders each year. Yet the figure would need to reach about 9 million for today's global migration rate to match the rate in the early twentieth century. So when people claim that the contemporary era is a new age of diaspora, they are usually referring to gross numbers rather than the overall rate of migration. And they are employing diaspora as a synonym for population movement in general rather than as a concept for making sense of certain kinds of migration.

International migration, moreover, is less open today than it was a century ago. In both Asia and the Atlantic world, the century beginning in the 1830s was the golden age of unrestricted mass migration. Most of the big receiving countries for European migrants, notably the United States, Canada, Australia, and New Zealand, imposed restrictions on immigration during and after World War I. Combined with the effects of the Great Depression and World War II, these measures brought the era of mass migration from Europe to an end. In Asia, likewise, the economic downturn and the outbreak of war in the 1930s signaled the end of the great cycle of open migration. Although the United States abolished its race-based quota system in 1965, inaugurating a new era of global immigration, international migration throughout the world is now regulated by vast state bureaucracies. The European

Union, to be sure, has opened its borders—but only for Europeans. The system of passports, visas, and border controls introduced in the restriction era is here to stay.

Nevertheless, contemporary migration has several characteristics that are strikingly new. Since about 1960, for the first time in history, half of all international migrants are women. Sex ratios varied in previous migrations, but male breadwinners were typically the first to set off, often embarking on temporary and cyclical journeys to supplement family income. Once migrants began to develop communities abroad, women evidently played as prominent a role as men. Without a rough demographic balance between the sexes, after all, no such community can emerge in the first place. But in the early stages of migration, women were usually the minority. They were discouraged, in most countries, from leaving home unless they were married. For young, single women, overseas migration was generally taboo (though the Irish in the late nineteenth century were exceptions to this rule). At the same time, much of the work available abroad—heavy, manual, unskilled—was for men only.

The equal sex ratios among migrants today do not necessarily signify a move toward gender equality, in either the sending or the receiving countries. Women are migrating in larger numbers because opportunity is constricted at home and demand for their labor is high in the service sector, menial work, and sweatshops of the host countries. They do the work that most native-born workers no longer wish to do. These women often migrate to support children or other family members left at home. Their migration can involve an extension of patriarchal family structures overseas rather than an escape from these constraints. Just as young Irish women in the nineteenth century were obliged by their parents to send back remittances from New York and Boston, many Latin American women today come to the United States with the primary intention of supporting their families at home.

The most significant new force in facilitating migration and diasporic connectivity today is technology. Innovations in transport and communication have enabled much faster and easier forms of migration. Since the advent of relatively inexpensive air travel on a mass scale in the 1970s, most long-distance migrants have traveled by plane rather than by boat or overland. It once took months to travel by ship from India to England, but now people can fly direct in less than ten hours. The availability of inexpensive international telephone calls from the 1980s on enabled much more frequent and efficient communication. And the emergence of the World Wide Web in the 1990s allowed migrants to stay in touch with their home communities and their fellow diasporans to an extent undreamed of before. How would a migrant a century ago—or even a decade ago—have responded if told she could call home on Skype?

The Internet, with its vast network of information and communication, is an almost perfect vehicle for propagating a sense of diaspora. Like the concept of diaspora, the Internet involves a network without centers based on multipolar rather than one-way connections. Almost every migrant group today defines itself online, using websites, blogs, chat rooms, and discussion groups to advance its cause. This kind of communication can sometimes facilitate what one scholar has aptly termed "long-distance nationalism"—a fervent, yet curiously abstract, type of political commitment in which support for the homeland emerges almost as a byproduct of the search for a meaningful life abroad. But this kind of sentiment is a variation on a well-established historical pattern: migrants have always found in diasporic nationalism a way not only to help their homelands but also to get ahead in their new hostlands.

Reaching out

Soon after Mary Robinson became president of Ireland in 1990, she lit a symbolic candle in the window of her official residence. The candle was to welcome anyone of Irish descent—recent emigrants as well as descendants of those who had left in the distant past—who wished to return to Ireland. Educated in the United States and well aware of the economic and political power of Irish Americans, Robinson delivered a speech called "Cherishing the Irish Diaspora" to a joint session of the Irish Parliament in 1995. The diaspora, she noted, had been born in tragedy and sorrow, but it had become one of Ireland's greatest treasures. When Article 2 of the Irish Constitution was revised in 1998 as part of the Belfast Agreement bringing peace to Northern Ireland, a clause was added stating that "the Irish nation cherishes its special affinity with people of Irish ancestry living abroad who share its cultural identity and heritage."

Robinson's call for cooperative projects between the Irish at home and abroad paid off during the era of the "Celtic Tiger" (1995–2007), a period of extraordinary, but in the end evanescent, economic growth. Many Irish migrants returned home during the boom, and for the first time in modern history the number of people entering the country exceeded the number who were leaving. During the severe economic recession that followed, however, Irish people began to leave again in large numbers, and even more would have left if they could have escaped the burden of debts accumulated during the boom. In 2011 Ireland began to issue new Certificates of Irish Heritage to anyone with at least one Irish ancestor. The government also declared that 2013 would be the "Year of the Gathering," an opportunity for all people who were "Irish born, Irish bred, or Irish in spirit" to contribute to the country's cultural and economic recovery.

The establishment of the Republic of Armenia in 1991 prompted similar initiatives. In 1998 President Robert Kocharian declared that Armenia would strengthen its links with the diaspora (*spurk* in Armenian). A special department within the Ministry of Foreign Affairs took charge of relations with people of Armenian origin living overseas. Some eight hundred delegates from fifty-two countries assembled in Yerevan for the first Armenia-Diaspora conference in 1999. Subsequent conferences were held in Yerevan in 2002 and 2006. In a further effort to secure overseas support, the Armenian Constitution was amended in 2008 to introduce a form of dual citizenship, including voting rights, for qualified people of Armenian origin abroad.

The Chinese government, likewise, has worked to foster stronger diasporic links in recent decades. Today, the number of "Overseas Chinese"—people of Chinese birth or descent living abroad, including foreign nationals—is estimated at 40 million. Indonesia, Thailand, Malaysia, Singapore, the United States, and Canada are the major locations. Smaller populations live in Peru, Vietnam, the Philippines, and Myanmar. Cities such as Vancouver, Sydney, and New York City have joined Singapore and Hong Kong in a global network bound together by enterprise and investment. In these cities, Chinese people from around the world, who have had no prior interaction with one another, find themselves in an immediately recognizable cultural setting—the new global Chinatown.

Aware of the considerable wealth of this international network, the Chinese government offers preferential treatment to overseas entrepreneurs interested in developing China's economy. The Overseas Chinese Affairs Office (OCAO), an administrative branch of the State Council, seeks to protect the rights and interests of the overseas Chinese, supports Chinese media and Chinese-language schools abroad, and promotes economic, scientific, and cultural exchange. Every Chinese municipality, autonomous region, and province (except Tibet) has its own OCAO branch. By some estimates, almost three-quarters of direct foreign investment in China now comes from Chinese overseas.

The People's Republic of China does not recognize dual nationality. Individuals of Chinese origin living abroad may apply for Chinese citizenship under certain conditions, but only if they are not citizens of their host countries. Yet the ever-expanding links between China and its overseas population are clearly producing a new, global sense of Chineseness that transcends national boundaries and citizenship status. Because so many overseas Chinese today receive their elementary and secondary education in China before they go abroad for the tertiary stage, they often retain a good deal of loyalty to the state and the Communist Party. Their foreign-born children attend OCAO-run summer camps, getting in touch with their Chinese roots before returning to their permanent homes overseas. Many of the new overseas Chinese cooperate closely with the government at home and lobby energetically in its interests. Back and forth movement, especially for business purposes, is increasingly common.

The Indian government reaches out to its diaspora in similar ways. Countries around the world with sizable and long-established Indian populations include Nepal, Malaysia, Myanmar, Singapore, South Africa, Mauritius, Trinidad and Tobago, and Fiji. Since World War II, Indians have migrated in large numbers to England and, since the 1960s, to the United States, Canada, and Australia. More recently, the oil-rich, labor-hungry countries of the Persian Gulf have been a major destination for Indian migrants, especially Muslims. Denied citizenship in these countries, the migrants tend to be short-term, with a stream of exploited workers steadily replenished by new arrivals. In the United States, by contrast, Indians are the best educated and most economically prosperous of all immigrant groups.

The Indian government offers a variety of incentives to its overseas population, seeking to enlist their economic support in return. In the late 1970s, the government introduced the category of Non-Resident Indians (NRIs) to classify Indian citizens and passport holders living permanently abroad. The more expansive category of Persons of Indian Origin (PIOs), introduced in 1999, included foreign nationals of Indian birth or ancestry (going back four generations). The PIO cards cost 15,000 rupees ($300) for adults and 7,500 rupees for minors and carry the right to enter India without a visa for fifteen years. In 1991, 1998, and 2000 the

Indian government tapped into overseas wealth by issuing a total of $12.3 billion in "diaspora bonds." A High Level Committee in 2000 outlined a global policy for the "Indian Diaspora" and, in 2003, the Ministry for Overseas Indian Affairs and the Federation of Indian Chambers of Commerce and Industry held the first annual Indian Diaspora Day.

In 2004 the Indian government created the category of Overseas Citizenship of India (OCI), open to all Indians abroad who had migrated after 1950 (except those who had departed from Pakistan and Bangladesh). Despite its name, OCI fell well short of dual citizenship, which is not permitted under the Indian constitution. It did, however, offer lifelong multiple entries into India without a visa. Those with OCI status could apply for citizenship after five years, provided they had spent at least one year in India, but they would have to give up their existing citizenship. Both PIOs and OCIs could pass through expedited immigration counters on arrival in India. They were exempt from a wide range of financial regulations and special charges imposed on foreigners, and they could take advantage of a variety of tax exemptions on income and investment.

Reaching out to the diaspora is also a central initiative of the African Union (AU). Founded in 2002 as a successor to the Organization of African Unity, the AU consists of fifty-four states— all countries on the continent except Morocco. Meeting in Addis Ababa in February 2003, the AU voted to amend its Constitutive Act to encourage members of "the African diaspora" to participate in the development of the Union. In Ghana, the following year, the AU representatives created the Diaspora African Forum (DAF) to facilitate this interaction. In April 2005 the AU adopted a definition of the "African diaspora" embracing all people of African descent or heritage living outside the continent, whatever their nationality or citizenship, who retained a connection with the continent and were willing to support the idea of African unity economically or politically.

The AU has sponsored two major conferences as part of this initiative. The First Conference of Intellectuals of Africa and the Diaspora (CIAD I), held in Senegal in 2004, hosted seven hundred intellectual and cultural figures from North, Central, and South America, the Caribbean, Europe, and the Arab world, as well as Africa. Leading African government officials also attended. The delegates supported a proposal by the president of Senegal, Abdulaye Wade, to confer on the African Diaspora the title "sixth region" of the AU (supplementing North, South, East, West, and Central Africa).

The second African diaspora conference (CIAD II) met in Salvador, Brazil, in 2006. This conference took as its topic "Africa in the Twenty-first Century: Integration and Renaissance." About 1,200 people attended the opening session, presided over by President Luiz Inacio Lula da Silva and featuring high-ranking

10. *Revelations*, by Alvin Ailey's American Dance Theater, tells the story of African American history from slavery to the present, celebrating the creative and unifying aspects of diaspora.

officials from several African countries, along with Kenya's Nobel Peace laureate, Wangari Maathai. The conference divided its main topic into six subthemes: Pan-Africanism, the contribution of intellectuals, relations between "Africa and its Diasporas," African identity in multicultural contexts, the place of Africa in the world, and science and technology. The legendary African American singer-songwriter Stevie Wonder set the tone by repeating the words spoken to him by his mother: "We should, we can, we must and we will."

The AU conferences inspired a proliferation of Pan-African organizations in the United States and elsewhere. Clearly, many people of African origin around the world continue to embrace elements of a Pan-African identity. The idea of diaspora can therefore be a powerful source of political mobilization. In 2012, for example, Haiti successfully applied for associate membership in the AU, the first non-African country to do so. Diaspora can also inspire great art, music, and literature. As an idea, it embraces themes of captivity and exile, but also salvation and redemption. Many African Americans have seen these two poles of the human experience as inseparable, believing that only the suffering of the chosen will redeem society as a whole. Diaspora, in this sense, can provide not simply a narrative of exploitation but also a source of unity and liberation.

Chapter 6
The future of diaspora

The idea of diaspora offers a powerful perspective on migration, based on the three interrelated dimensions of movement, connectivity, and return. Diaspora illuminates numerous aspects of Jewish, African, Irish, and Asian history, but it can also be applied to many other migrant groups across time and space. The history of the Sikhs and the Kurds, for example, fits well within the framework of diaspora, as does the history of the Roma ("Gypsies") in certain respects. In the early modern period, likewise, the dispersal of some 200,000 French Huguenots can be understood from a diasporic perspective. Readers may wish to consider how well the framework applies to other groups and eras, including patterns of dispersal specific to Muslims, or sustained periods of intense migration in the context of the collapse of state power, as in early medieval Europe. Because diaspora has limited explanatory power in the absence of states and homelands, it is more relevant to ancient and especially modern history than to other periods. And because most conceptions of diaspora are concerned with nation states in particular, the term has a distinctively contemporary valence.

Two contrary versions of the idea are currently in play, depending on who is using the term and for what purpose. One approach supports nationalist history, whereas the other can have the opposite effect. Diaspora in the first sense has a tendency to flatten out differences, to homogenize, to reduce complexity and diversity to a single type. In its second, more critical sense, however, diaspora can be used to draw important analytical distinctions between different kinds of human experience. Any concluding assessment of diaspora and its future relevance must take these contradictory tendencies into account.

There are significant pitfalls in using diaspora without careful reflection. It has become a trendy word in both popular and academic usage. Diaspora has a nice ring to it: the word rolls easily off the tongue, adding apparent substance to what may actually be rather empty claims. Unless the term is used with conscious meaning, it can signify little. Even when used reflectively, it can homogenize and oversimplify. A single event or episode—the Babylonian captivity, the Atlantic slave trade, the Irish famine, the Armenian genocide—can too easily come to stand as a surrogate for a group's entire migration history. And because the idea of diaspora involves particular forms of suffering, it can result in facile historical analogies concerning racism or genocide. Not every form of anti-immigrant prejudice involves race, and not every migration is an exodus. Another pitfall is the tendency to take the views of a vocal elite as typical of all members of a group they claim to represent. A diasporic approach can sometimes result in a kind of large-scale national history.

In this approach, globally scattered people whose ancestors happen to originate in a single place are endowed with common characteristics on that basis alone. They become, in effect, members of a "transnational nation," with their supposedly timeless attributes constituting a common culture, regardless of where the migrants settled. How helpful is it to talk of "the Irish diaspora" or "the African diaspora" if all one means by these terms is the number of people globally who claim Irish or African descent? Do such people, living in widely different settings around the world, necessarily share common characteristics? To speak of an African or an Irish diaspora in this sense, and to count numbers accordingly, is to fall into the trap of "essentialism." Migration history becomes little more than the story of fixed and inherent cultural essences transplanted without change from one part of the world to others. Diaspora becomes a form of biological destiny.

One of the most striking ways in which deploying the idea of diaspora can result in national history writ large is through the outreach efforts by governments to their overseas populations. For all the talk of the demise of nation states in the age of globalization, governments that reach out to "their" diasporas are clearly augmenting their economic power. They are even beginning to extend their sovereignty by offering concessions on citizenship or voting rights to overseas populations in return for political or economic support. Diaspora can therefore serve to strengthen rather than undermine nation states. China and India, in particular, have the potential to become new supernations in this way.

Those who use the category of diaspora for scholarly purposes will remain critical of approaches that homogenize diverse populations. To offset this tendency, it is helpful for the category to include a comparative dimension. Migrants who originate in the same countries have significantly different histories abroad, depending on where they settle. To be Irish in Britain or Australia is not the same as being Irish in America. Afro-Caribbean culture differs starkly from African American culture. Jamaicans in London have radically different experiences from Jamaicans in New York City or Kingston. The comparative method seeks out these differences as well as the similarities. But it is not well suited to analyzing dynamic forms of demographic, economic, political, and cultural interaction. These are the domain of diaspora par excellence. The best approach to migration history integrates a comparative dimension into a larger framework of diaspora.

Diaspora in its second sense embraces but moves beyond the comparative method. By examining interaction as well as variation, this approach presents a clear alternative to the homogenizing, quasi-nationalist model. Far from classifying people by nation or lumping them into supernations, it undermines the supposedly fixed and natural relationship between identity and place. This approach is powerfully "anti-essentialist," rejecting the notion that people, nations, or races have characteristics or inner essences that stand outside historical time or are grounded in geographical territory. Diaspora, understood in this way, does not respect boundaries. In the language of cultural studies, it deals more with "routes" than with "roots." The emphasis is on movement and connections rather than origins. Going beyond the simple polarity of homeland and hostland, this approach is less interested in where people come from than in how they travel and interact.

Diaspora in this sense greatly enriches our understanding of migration. The field of migration history deals, by definition, with movement from one place to another. Yet for the modern and contemporary eras at least, it is strongly nation-based. Its vocabulary is organized around the dualities of push and pull, emigration and immigration, uprooting and transplantation, usually applied to the relationship between one sending country and one receiving country. The concept of diaspora can transcend this limited perspective, revealing multifaceted patterns of interaction and exchange.

Migration was the greatest centrifugal force in history, scattering people all over the earth and giving rise to an astonishing variety of languages, religions, and cultures. Only recently has it become a potential source of convergence, bringing people back together and breaking down the artificial boundaries that earlier migrations created. In Asia, internal and external migrations have recently unleashed the fastest and largest wave of urbanization in history. Eleven of the world's seventeen megacities—those with populations of more than 10 million—are located on that continent. Vast, cosmopolitan cities of this kind are the locations for most of the world's diasporic populations today. New models of sovereignty are emerging, involving dual, multiple, or flexible citizenship. Those who are working to define these new forms of affiliation and belonging could do worse than study the concept of diaspora.

As in previous eras of history, diaspora offers a framework for understanding the world created by migration. As a concept, it is both powerful and empowering; migrants and governments deploy it for their own purposes and reap the dividends it has to offer. The job of scholars and students is to delineate the possible meanings of diaspora and to determine its utility. There is considerable merit in this enterprise. But if a given group chooses to define itself as a diaspora for its own purposes, who is the author of a short introduction to disagree? People will always find what they are looking for in the idea of diaspora. And because people's needs change over time, members of the same group may find the idea more or less appealing in different periods. Diaspora is a powerful source of cultural and political mobilization, and it will become even more powerful as migrants and their descendants continue to forge links among themselves and with their homelands.

According to the "law of the third generation" once proposed by a historian of American immigration, the grandchildren of immigrants seek to remember what the children of immigrants tried to forget. Those who make the journey often try to release their children (the second generation) from the dead hand of the past, but the members of the third generation may wish to embrace that past as they seek to discover who they are. This theory has a certain validity, especially in the case of American history, where migrants often encouraged their children to cast off their old-world language and culture, or were forced to do so. The position of the second generation in today's world of rapid communication and flexible citizenship is more complex and ambiguous than in the past. But for all who seek to discover where they came from, and to understand what they have become, diaspora will retain a powerful attraction.

Further reading

General works

Cohen, Robin. *Global Diasporas: An Introduction*. 2d ed. New York: Routledge, 2008.

Dufoix, Stéphane. *La dispersion: Un histoire des usages du mot diaspora*. Paris: Éditions Amsterdam, 2012.

Dufoix, Stéphane. *Diasporas*. Berkeley: University of California Press, 2009.

Knott, Kim, and Seán McLoughlin, eds. *Diasporas: Concepts, Intersections, and Identities*. New York: Zed Books, 2010.

Chapter 1: What is diaspora?

Baumann, Martin. "Diaspora: Genealogies of Semantics and Transcultural Comparison." *Numen* 47.3 (2000): 313–37.

Brubaker, Rogers. "The 'Diaspora' Diaspora." *Ethnic and Racial Studies* 28.1 (2005): 1–19.

Clifford, James. "Diasporas." *Cultural Anthropology* 9 (1994): 302–38.

Hall, Stuart. "Cultural Identity and Diaspora." In *Identity: Community, Culture, Difference*, ed. Jonathan Rutherford, 222–37. London: Lawrence and Wishart, 1990.

Safran, William. "Diasporas in Modern Societies: Myths of Homeland and Return." *Diaspora* 1 (Spring 1991): 83–99.

Chapter 2: Migration

Amrith, Sunil S. *Migration and Diaspora in Modern Asia*. Cambridge: Cambridge University Press, 2010.

Brown, Judith M. *Global South Asians: Introducing the Modern Diaspora.* Cambridge: Cambridge University Press, 2006.

Gomez, Michael. *Reversing Sail: A History of the African Diaspora.* New York: Cambridge University Press, 2005.

Kenny, Kevin. "Diaspora and Comparison: The Global Irish as a Case Study." *Journal of American History* 90 (June 2003): 134–62.

King, Russell, ed. *Atlas of World Migration.* Buffalo, NY: Firefly Books, 2007.

Manning, Patrick. *Migration in World History.* New York: Routledge, 2005.

Northrup, David. *Indentured Labor in the Age of Imperialism, 1834–1922.* Cambridge: Cambridge University Press, 1995.

Olson, Steve. *Mapping Human History: Genes, Race, and Our Common Origins.* Boston: Mariner Books, 2002.

Chapter 3: Connections

Gilroy, Paul. *The Black Atlantic: Modernity and Double Consciousness.* Cambridge, MA: Harvard University Press, 1993.

Gomez, Michael. *Exchanging our Country Marks: The Transformation of African Identities in the Colonial and Antebellum South.* Chapel Hill: University of North Carolina Press, 1998.

Gomez, Michael. *Reversing Sail: A History of the African Diaspora.* New York: Cambridge University Press, 2005.

Parekh, Bikhu. "Some Reflections on the Hindu Diaspora." *New Community* 20 (July 1994): 603–20.

Sheffer, Gabriel. *Diaspora Politics: At Home Abroad.* New York: Cambridge University Press, 2003.

Shepperson, George. "The African Diaspora—or the African Abroad." *African Forum* 2 (1966): 76–93.

Chapter 4: Return

Aviv, Caryn, and David Shneer. *New Jews: The End of the Jewish Diaspora.* New York: New York University Press, 2005.

Barrett, Leonard E. Sr. *The Rastafarians.* Twentieth anniversary ed. Boston: Beacon Press, 1997.

Boyarin, Daniel, and Jonathan Boyarin. "Diaspora: Generation and the Ground of Jewish Identity." *Critical Inquiry* 19 (Summer 1993): 693–725.

Bradley, Lloyd. *This Is Reggae Music: The Story of Jamaica's Music*. New York: Grove Press, 2001.

Gelvin, James L. *The Israel-Palestine Conflict: One Hundred Years of War*. 2d ed. New York: Cambridge University Press, 2007.

O'Brien Chang, Kevin, and Wayne Chen. *Reggae Routes: The Story of Jamaican Music*. Philadelphia, PA: Temple University Press, 1998.

Sidbury, James. *Becoming African in America: Race and Nation in the Early Black Atlantic*. New York: Oxford University Press, 2009.

Smith, Charles D. *Palestine and the Arab-Israeli Conflict: A History with Documents*. 7th ed. Boston: Bedford/St. Martin's, 2010.

Chapter 5: A global concept

Aviv, Caryn, and David Shneer. *New Jews: The End of the Jewish Diaspora*. New York: New York University Press, 2005.

Castles, Stephen, and Mark J. Miller. *The Age of Migration: International Population Movements in the Modern World*. 4th ed. London: Guildford Press, 2009.

Gitelman, Zvi. "The Decline of the Diaspora Jewish Nation: Boundaries, Content, and Jewish Identity." *Jewish Social Studies*, New Series 4 (Winter 1998): 112–32.

Koser, Khalid. *International Migration: A Very Short Introduction*. Oxford: Oxford University Press, 2007.

Tölölyan, Khachig. "Rethinking Diaspora(s): Stateless Power in the Transnational Moment." *Diaspora* 5 (Spring 1996): 3–36.

Index

A

Abraham, 3
ACS. *See* American Colonization Society
Afghanistan, 94
Africa
  diaspora and, 42–44, 54–60
  flag for, 59
  migration from, 24, 26, 27–28, 47–48
  reggae in, 86
  return to, 55, 56, 61, 77–81, 83–84
  See also specific countries in Africa
African Americans, 55–56, 78–79, 80, *103*
Africans, 8–9, 24–28, 42–43, 47–48. *See also* Pan-Africanism; slavery
African Union (AU), 102–4
Agudas, 79
Alexander II (tsar), 23
Alexander the Great, 21
aliyah, 62, 64, 65
Allen, Richard, 78
Alpha Blondy, 86
Alvin Ailey's American Dance Theater, *103*

AME. *See* Bethel African Methodist Episcopal Church
American Colonization Society (ACS), 78–79
Amin, Idi, 91
Arab-Israeli War, 67
Arabs, 62, 63, 65, 66, 67–70
Arch of Titus, 3, *4*
Ark of the Covenant, 55, 73, 81
Armenia, 6–7, 99–100
Armenians, 7–8
Armstrong, Louis, 9
Ashkenazim, 21, 22
Asia. *See specific Asian countries*
Assam, 89
Assyrians, 3
AU. *See* African Union
Australia, 38
  Chinese in, 37
  immigration restriction in, 51, 96
  Indians in, 91, 101
  Irish in, 29, 31, 42, 53, 107
  refugees in, 93
Australopithecus, 17, 18

B

Babylon, 3, 5, 41, 46, 83
Babylonian captivity, 2, 3, 5, 16, 106

"Back to Africa" movements,
    77–84,
Balfour, Arthur, 63
Balfour Declaration, 63
Belfast Agreement, 99
Ben-Gurion, David, 65, *66*
Beta Israel, 73, 74
Bethel African Methodist Episcopal
    Church (AME), 58, 78
bhangra music, 85–86
Bible, 2, 40. *See also specific*
    Biblical texts
birds of passage, 33
Black Star Line, 59, 78
Blyden, Edward, 55, 79
boat people, 93
Bob Marley and the Wailers,
    84–85, 86
bonded laborers, 32–39, 48–50
Brazil, 26, 48, 79
Brigadier Jerry, 85
Britain, 38
    Asians in, 44, 86, 101
    black colonization and, 77–78
    East African Asians in, 90, 91
    Irish in, 31, 42
    Irish famine and, 31–32, 47
    music in, 85–86,
    slavery and, 48
    Zionism and, 63
British Empire, 34, 48, 53, 54
British Guiana, 48–49, 50
Burma, 34–35, 50, 89. *See also*
    Myanmar
Burning Spear, 85
Byzantium, 7

C

call-and-response, 56–57
Cambodia, 92, 93
Cameroon, 24
Camps des Noirs, 48
Canada, 38, *96*, 91, 93, 100, 101
candomblé, 57

Caribbean, 42
    Asian migrant workers in, 35, 49
    decolonization, 55, 56
    intellectuals, 59
    music, 85
    religion, 43, 57
    slavery, 26, 27, 43
caste system, 44, 49
Catherine the Great, 23
Catholicism, 29, 42, 47
Celtic Tiger, 61, 99
Certificates of Irish Heritage, 99
Césaire, Aimé, 59
Ceylon, 34–35, 90
Chettiar caste, 52, 89
Chile, 70
China, 32, 54, 88, 100, 101, 107
Chinese
    ethnic, 88–89, 92–93
    migrants, 32–33, 37, 38
    overseas, 44, 51, *51*, 88, 89, 92–93,
        100–101
    prejudice against, 44, 88–89, 92
    refugees, 92–93
    settlements by, 50–51, 52, 100
Christianity, 22, 42, 43, 54–55,
        57, 58. *See also* Bible; *specific*
        branches of Christianity
CIAD. *See* Conference of Intellectuals
    of Africa and the Diaspora
Cilicia, 7
citizenship
    Chinese, 100–1, 107
    dual, 87, 100, 102, 109
    flexible, 87, 108–9
    Indian, 89, 90, 102, 107
    in Netherlands, 91
    for Palestinian refugees, 68–69, 70
    U.S., 42, 44
Clay, Henry, 78
Conference of Intellectuals of
    Africa and the Diaspora
    (CIAD), 103–4
coolies, 35, 38
Cotton Kingdom, 26

Count Ossie (Oswald Williams), 84
Cuba, 26, 27, 49, 57
Cuffe, Paul, 58, 78, 80

D

DAF. *See* Diaspora African Forum
Damas, Léon, 59
Dan, tribe of, 73
Delany, Martin, 80
Democratic Republic of Congo, 94
Deposito de Cimarrones, 49
de Valera, Éamon, 53
Dhangars, 49
dharma (duty), 44–45
diaspeirein, 2, 3–4, 5
diasporá, 2, 3–4
*Diaspora: A Journal of
    Transnational Studies*, 10
Diaspora African Forum (DAF), 102
diaspora bonds, 76–77, 101–2
Diop, Alioune, 59
dreadlocks, 82–83, 84
Du Bois, W. E. B., 43, 58
Dutch Guiana, 50, 91

E

East Africa, 35, 90
Economic Pressure, 30
Egypt, 3, 7, 8, 67–68, 69
Epicurus, 2
Equiano, Olaudah, 54
Eretz Israel (Land of Israel),
    3, 65
eschatology, 5
essentialism, 106–7, 108
Ethiopia, 18, 19, 54, 81–82, 83, 102
    Jews in, 73–74, 75
Ethiopian Orthodox Church, 82
Ethiopian World Federation
    (EWF), 83
Euphrates River, 41
EWF. *See* Ethiopian World
    Federation

Exile, 8, 40, 104
    of Africans, 55, 77, 82, 83
    of Indians, 44, 45
    of Irish, 28, 31, 40, 42, 47, 53, 61
    of Jews, 1, 2, 3, 5, 22, 23–24, 31, 41,
        46, 53, 65, 72
    of Palestinians, 70
Exodus, 3, 4, 8–9, 42, 55

F

falasha (landless), 73
Falash Mura, 74
famine, 28–29, 30–32, 42
Fanon, Frantz, 60
Fiji, 34, 35–36, 44, 49, 50, 91
First Congress of Negro Writers
    and Artists, 59
Freedmen's Bureau, 80
Freedom's Journal, 79
Freetown, 78

G

galut, 5, 22
ganja, 83
Garvey, Marcus, 58–59, 78, 80–81, 84
Gaza Strip, 67, 68, 69–70
Ge'ez, 73
Genesis, 3, 4, 41
genocide, 8, 30, 31, 106
Germany, 18, 21, 22, 23, 46, 94
Ghana, 58, 79, 102
Glissant, Édouard, 59
"Go Down Moses," 8–9
Great Depression, 88, 89, 96
Great Flood, 41
Great Migration, 55
Greece, 46
guano mines, 49
"Gypsies" (Roma), 105

H

Hadar, 18
Hadrian (emperor), 3

Haiti, 26, 43, 57, 104
Hanuman, 44, 45
Harare, 86
Herzl, Theodor, 62, 65, *66*
Hindus, 44, 49
Hoa, 92
Holocaust, 8, 24, 65, 72
Holy Spirit, 57
Homo Erectus, 18
Homo Sapiens, 17, 19, 20
Hong Kong, 37, 93, 100
Howell, Leonard, 82

I

IDPs. *See* internally displaced people
Ilawi, 85
Indentured workers, 35–36, *36*, 37, 38, 48–50, 54
India
    citizenship in, 90, 102, 107
    diaspora bonds of, 101–2
    migration from, 32–33, 34–36, *36*, 38, 49
    music from, 85–86
    return to, 35, 37, 45, 90
Indian Diaspora Day, 102
Indian Ocean, 24, 25
Indians, 35, 44, 48, 50, 89–91, 101
Indonesia, 35, 51, 88, 89, 100
Inquisition, 22, 24
internally displaced people (IDPs), 94
International Migrants Day, 95
Iran, 7, 8, 94
Iraq, 41, 48, 67, 68, 69, 94
Ireland
    as British colony, 28
    as Celtic Tiger, 61, 99
    famine in, 28–29, 30–32
    migration from, 28–30, *30*, 31–32
    Northern, 99
Irgun, 64–65
Irish
    as exiles, 28, 31, 40, 42, 47, 53
    migrants, 28–30, *30*, 31–32, 42

    nationalism of, 53–54
    overseas, 29, 31, 42, 46–47
    prejudice against, 42, 47
    return of, 47, 61, 98–99
Irish Constitution, 99
Isabella (queen), 22
Isaiah, 72, 83–84
Israel, 5, 21
    Arabs in, 66, 67, 69, 70
    attack on, 67
    Declaration of Independence, 65–66, *66*, 67, 72
    diaspora bonds of, 76–77
    as *Eretz Israel*, 3, 65
    Independence Day, 67
    Law of Return, 71, 72–76
    repatriation to, 72–74, *75*
    state of, 65
    See also Palestine
Italians, 33, 38

J

Jabotinsky, Vladimir, 64–65
Jaffa, *68*
Jah Love Muzik International, 85
Jamaica, 41, 48, 58–59, 82, 83, 85
Java Man, 18
Jeremiah, 40, 46, 76
Jerusalem, 3, 21, 46, 62
Jewish National Fund, 64
Jewish People's Council, *66*
Jews
    Ashkenazi, 21, 22
    assimilation of, 40, 46, 52–53, 76, 77
    in Babylon, 2, 3, 5, 40, 46
    as exiles, 1, 3, 5, 22, 23–24, 31, 41, 46, 53
    homeland for, 62, 63, 65–66
    Iberian, 22, 24
    identity of, 72, 76
    Law of Return and, 71, 72–76
    migration of, 2–3, 20–24, 45, 62–66, 72–76
    overseas, 45–46, 52–53, 64, 71, 76–77

Palestine and, 45, 62–72
population of, 76
prejudice against, 22–24, 62, 65
return of, 62–66, 72–76, *75*
Sephardic, 21, 22
Soviet, 74, 76
Yemenite, 72
Johnson, Lynton Kwesi, 85
Jordan, 67, 68, 69, 70, 94
Joseph, 3
Judah, 3, 21, 62

K

kangani, 34–35, 37
Keating, Seán, *30*
Kebra Negast, 73, 81
Kenya, 34, 90
kibbutzim (communal farming
    settlements), 64
King, Martin Luther, Jr., 56
Kingston, 82
Kocharian, Robert, 99
kumina, 57, 84
Kurds, 7, 105

L

Latin America, 37, 42–43, 57, 97
Law of Entry, 74
Law of Return, 71, 72–76
law of the third generation, 109
Lebanon, 68, 69, 70
Levi, Barrington, 85
Liberia, 55, 79, 80
Livingston, Bunny (Bunny Wailer),
    84–85
Lucy, 18

M

Maathai, Wangari, 104
Makonnen, Tafari, 81
Malaya, 34, 35, 51
Malaysia, 50, 88, 93, *93*, 100, 101

Mandate of the League of Nations,
    64, 67
manumission, 43
marijuana, 83
Marley, Bob, 84–85, 86
Mauritius, 34, 35, 37, 48–49, 50,
    101
Menelik, 73, 81
Messiah, 63
Middle Passage, 27–28, 42, 55, 56
migration
    contemporary, 96–97
    diaspora and, 6, 9, 16, 20–21, 24,
        29, 39, 108–9
    involuntary, 38–39, 94
    prehistoric, 17, 18
    rate, 95–96
    regulation of, 96–97
    repeat, 87–91
    restrictions on, 44, 51, 96
    return, 3, 5, 6, 7, 13, 20–21, 22, 33,
        34, 35, 37, 40, 44, 45, 46, 47,
        53, 55, 58, 60, 61–62, 71, 72–84,
        88–89, 90, 98–99
    sex ratios in, 27, 46, 50, 97
    short-term, 33, 50, 101
    See also specific nationalities
Mitchel, John, 31
mitochondria, 17
Modibo, Askia, 86
Monroe, James, 79
Monrovia, 79
Moses, 3, 22
music, 56–57, 84–86
Myanmar, 94, 100, 101. *See also*
    Burma
Mystic Revelation of Rastafari, 84

N

NAACP. *See* National Association
    for the Advancement of
    Colored People
Naipaul, V.S., 45
Natal, 35, 37, 49

National Association for the Advancement of Colored People (NAACP), 58
National Convention of Men of Color, 80
nationalism, 6, 12, 52, 106
   African American, 79, 80
   Irish, 53–54
   long-distance, 98
   Palestinian, 71
   Pan-African, 86
   Zionism as, 62, 63
Naturei Karta, 71
Neanderthals, 18–19
Nebuchadnezzar II (king), 3, 82
Négritude, 59–60
Negro World, 59
Netherlands, 22, 91
the new historians, 71
New York City, 51, *51*, 53, 77, 79, 100
New Zealand, 29, 38, 91, 96
Niger, Paul, 59
Nigeria, 24
nigger yards, 48–49
Non-Resident Indians (NRIs), 101
North Africa, 25
Northern Ireland, 29, 99
Northern Kingdom, 3
Nova Scotia, 77
NRIs. *See* Non-Resident Indians
nyabinghi, 84

O

OCAO. *See* Overseas Chinese Affairs Office
OCI. *See* Overseas Citizenship of India
Old Testament, 42, 43
olim, 62, 64, 65, 72, 74
Operation Moses, 73–74
Operation on Wings of Eagles, 72
Operation Solomon, 74, *75*
Organization of African Unity, 102

Ottoman Empire, 8, 62, 63
Overseas Chinese Affairs Office (OCAO), 100
Overseas Citizenship of India (OCI), 102

P

Pakistan, 91, 94, 102
Pale of Settlement, 23
Palestine, 7, 21, 45, 46, 62–72, *68*
Palestinian Liberation Organization (PLO), 71
Pan-Africanism, 43, 48, 58–59, 86, 104
Parnell, Charles Stewart, 53
Partition Plan, UN, 67
Peking Man, 18
Pentateuch, 4
Perry, Lee "Scratch" ("The Upsetter"), 85
Persia, 6, 7
Persian Gulf, 101
Persians, 3
persons of concern, 94
Persons of Indian Origin (PIOs), 101, 102
Peru, 37, 49, 51, 100
Phytophthora infestans. *See* famine
Pinnacle, 82–83
PIOs. *See* Persons of Indian Origin
PLO. *See* Palestinian Liberation Organization
Poland, 64
Portugal, 22, 23, 52
Presbyterians, 29
Promised Land, 3, 63, 81–82
Protestantism, 43, 57–58
Psalms, 41, 54–55, 82, 85

R

race, 17, 43, 56, 60, 106, 108
racism, 33, 40, 42, 56, 85, 106

raggamuffin (ragga), 85
Rama IV (king), 88
Ramayana, 44–45
Rangoon, 50, 89
Rastafari, 41, 55, 59, 81–85
Ras Tafari, 81
Reb Arelach, 71
Reconstruction, 80
refugees, 87
  Afghan, 94
  Cambodian, 93
  Chinese, 92–93, *93*
  classification as, 68–69, 92, 94
  Iraqi, 94
  organizations for, 68–69, 70, 92,
    93–94
  Palestinian, 67–70, *68*
  population of, 94
  Vietnamese, 93
  World Refugee Day, 93
reggae, 56, 81, 84–85
religions. *See specific religions*
Republic of Armenia, 7, 99–100
Republic of Liberia, 55, 79, 80
Réunion, 34, 50
Revelation 5:2–5, 82
Revelations (Alvin Ailey's), *103*
Revisionist Zionism, 64
Rhodesia, 86
Robeson, Paul, 9
Robinson, Mary, 98–99
Roma ("Gypsies"), 105
Roman, Charles Victor, 55
Roman Catholics, 29, 47, 79
Romans, 3, *4*
Rothschild, Walter, 63
Roumain, Jacques, 59
Russia, 23, 46, 63, 64, 76,
Russian Republic of Armenia, 8
Russwurm, John, 79

S

Saigon, 92
Second Temple, 3, *4*, 21, 46, 65

Selassie, Haile (emperor), 73, 81,
  82, 83, 84, 86
Senegal, 59, 103
Senghor, Léopold, 59
sensimilla, 83
Sephardim, 21, 22
Septuagint, 4, 5
Shamir, Yitzhak, 74
Shanghai, 54
al-Shatat (displacement,
  expulsion), 70
Sheba, Queen of, 73, 81
Siam, 88
Sierra Leone, 77–78
Sikhs, 7, 105
da Silva, Luiz Inacio Lula, 103
Singapore, 51, 100, 101
Sister Netifa, 85
Six-Day War, 69
slavery, 8
  abolition of, 48
  Arab, *25*, 25–26
  Atlantic, 25
  in Brazil, 26, 48
  in the Caribbean, 26, 27, 48
  Christianity and, 42, 43, 57
  diaspora and, 9, 24, 26–28, 43,
    48, 56
  diversity in, 43, 47–48
  Sierra Leone and, 77–78
  in U.S., 8–9, 26–27, 43
Slavs, 33
Solomon, 3, 73, 81
Somalia, 94
South Africa, 34, 35, 38, 44, 101
South America, 26–27, 48
Soviet Socialist Republic of
  Armenia, 7
Soviet Union, 74–76, 94
Spain, 21, 24, 52
Sri Lanka, 34–35, 90
statelessness, 65
Steel Pulse, 85
Sudan, 73–74
Suez Canal, 63

Suharto, General, 89
suicide, 49, *56*
Sumatra, 35, *36*, 37
supernaturalism, 57
Suriname, 35, 44, 50, 91
Syria, 65, 67, 68, 69, 70, 94

T

Tabom, 79
Talmud, 46
Tamils, 52, 90
Tanzania, 34, 90
Tel Aviv, *66*, *68*
Temple, 3, 41, 45, 82. *See also*
      Second Temple
Ten Commandments, 55
Thailand, 51, 88, 93, 100
Thucydides, 2
Tölölyan, Khachig, 10
Torah, 45, 62
Tosh, Peter, 84–85
Tower of Babel, 41
Trinidad, 83
      Indians in, 35, 37, 44, 45, 50, 57, 101
Tulsidas, 44
Twelve Tribes of Israel, 85

U

Uganda, 34, *62*, 90, 91
Ulster, 29
UNHCR. *See* United Nations High
      Commissioner for Refugees
UNIA. *See* United Negro
      Improvement Association
United Nations General Assembly,
      95
United Nations High
      Commissioner for Refugees
      (UNHCR), 68–69, 92, 93–94
United Nations Relief and Works
      Agency for Palestine Refugees
      in the Near East (UNRWA),
      69, 70

United Negro Improvement
      Association (UNIA), 58–59
United States (U.S.)
      African Americans in, 8–9, 26–27,
            43 55–56, 78–79, 80, *103*
            (*see also* United States [U.S.],
            slavery in)
      Armenians in, 7, 8
      Cambodians in, 93
      Chinese in, 44, 51, *51*, 100
      citizenship, 42, 44
      Civil War, 27, 80
      immigration restrictions by, 44,
            51, 96
      Indians in, 101
      Irish in, 29, 31, 32, 42, 46–47, 53
      Jews in, 22, 23, 46, 53, 63, 64, 76
      migration to, 95–96
      population growth, 96
      Revolution, 58, 77
      slavery in, 8–9, 26–27, 43
      Vietnamese in, 93
UN Partition Plan, 67
UNRWA. *See* United Nations Relief
      and Works Agency for Palestine
      Refugees in the Near East
urbanization, 108

V

Vietnam, 88, 92–93, *93*, 100
vodun (voodoo), 57

W

Wade, Abdulaye, *103*
West Africa, 47, 48, 78, 79, 80, 86
West Bank, 67–68, 69, 70
West Central Africa, 47
Williams, Eric, 83
Williams, Oswald (Count Ossie), 84
women
      employment of, 50, 97
      contemporary international
            migration and, 97

as prostitutes, 37
slavery and, 25–26
violence against, 50, 89
Wonder, Stevie, 104
World Refugee Day, 93
World Zionist Organization,
   64

Y

Yawm al-Nakba (day of
   catastrophe), 67

Year of the Gathering, 99
Yerevan, 99–100

Z

za-avah, 4, 5, 22
Zangwill, Israel, 62
Zanzibar, *25*
Zephaniah, Benjamin, 85
Zimbabwe, 86
Zionism, 62–67, 71
Zionist Congress, 62

BORDERS
A Very Short Introduction
Alexander C. Diener and Joshua Hagen

This *Very Short Introduction* challenges the perception of borders as passive lines on a map, revealing them instead to be integral forces in the economic, social, political, and environmental processes that shape our lives. Highlighting the historical development and continued relevance of borders, Diener and Hagen offer a powerful counterpoint to the idea of an imminent borderless world, underscoring the impact borders have on a range of issues, such as economic development, inter- and intra-state conflict, global terrorism, migration, nationalism, international law, environmental sustainability, and natural resource management. They demonstrate how and why borders have been, are currently, and will undoubtedly remain hot topics across the social sciences and in the global headlines for years to come.

"From private gated communities to fenced national borders and from gerrymandered electoral districts to bounded fiscal spaces, we all live with (and against) barriers. This lively, brief, current, impressively comprehensive and theoretically as well as philosophically inclusive 'introduction' is much more than that—it's terrific coverage."

Harm de Blij, John A. Hannah Professor,
Michigan State University

www.oup.com/uk/isbn/978-0-19-973150-3

INTERNATIONAL MIGRATION
A Very Short Introduction
Khalid Koser

International migration is an issue of intense public and political concern. How closely linked are migrants with terrorist organizations? What factors lie behind the dramatic increase in the number of woman migrating? This *Very Short Introduction* looks at the global phenomenon of human migration—both legal and illegal-revealing how migration actually presents opportunities that must be taken advantage of in light of the current economic climate. The author debunks myths such as the claim that migrants take jobs away from local workers, or that they take advantage of health care systems. He reveals why society as we now know it could not function without them. Using interviews with migrants from around the world, the author presents the human side of topics such as asylum and refugees, human trafficking, migrant smuggling, development, and the international labor force.

www.oup.com/uk/isbn/978-0-19-929801-3